PRACTICE – ASSESS – DIAGNOSE

180 Days of SOCIAL STUDIES
for Fifth Grade

D1216423

Authors

Catherine Cotton; Patricia Elliott M.A.; Melanie Joye, M.Ed.

SHELL EDUCATION

Publishing Credits

Corinne Burton, M.A.Ed., *Publisher*
Conni Medina, M.A.Ed., *Managing Editor*
Emily R. Smith, M.A.Ed., *Content Director*
Veronique Bos, *Creative Director*

Developed and Produced by

Focus Strategic Communications, Inc.

Project Manager: Adrianna Edwards
Editor: Ron Edwards, Kate Revington
Designer and Compositor: Tracy Westell
Proofreader: Audrey Dorsch
Photo Researcher: Paula Joiner
Art: Deborah Crowle, Tracy Westell

Image Credits

Image credits: cover, Detail of "Lewis & Clark at Three Forks" by Edgar Samuel Paxson (Public Domain), Wikimedia Commons; p.22 (top), p.23 By Aetzkorn (Own work) [Public domain], via Wikimedia Commons; p.26 By User:Nikater [Public domain], via Wikimedia Commons; p.33 Library of Congress, Rare Book and Special Collections Division, The Hans P. Kraus Collection of Sir Francis Drake; p.34 New York State Museum. Annual Report. Albany: University of the State of New York, 1902; p.35 The Graphics Fairy (www.thegraphicsfairy.com); p.37 Timewatch Images/ Alamy; p.39 Library of Congress [LC-USZ62-59702]; p.40 Colin Faulkingham/Wikimedia Commons; p.42 (top) Library of Congress [HABS MD,4-BALT,5–19]; p.42 (bottom) Library of Congress [HABS MD,4-BALT,5- (sheet 1 of 11); p.45 Library of Congress [LC-USZ62-45595]; p.47 (top left) SV Resolution at the English language Wikipedia, via Wikimedia Commons; p.47 (top center), p.47 (top right), p.47 (bottom right), p.96, p.143, p.169 (bottom), p.190 Science History Images/Alamy; p.47 (bottom left) Library of Congress, Geography and Map Division; p.49 Benson John Lossing, ed. Harper's Encyclopedia of United States History (vol. 10) (New York, NY: Harper and Brothers, 1912). Retrieved January 30, 2018; p.50 Library of Congress [LC-USZC4-4188]; p.54 Maury, Matthew Fontaine. Maury's New Elements of Geography for Primary and Intermediate Classes. New York: American Book Company, 1907. 28, 29; p.55 Library of Congress Geography and Map Division; p.56 solepsizm/Shutterstock; p.58 Bryant, William Cullen, and Gay, Sydney Howard. A Popular History of the United States. New York: Scribner, Armstrong, and Company, 1876; p.59 Library of Congress [LC-USZ61-206]; p.60 Library of Congress [LC-USZ62-120506]; p.61 Library of Congress [LC-USZ2-2452]; p.63 Library of Congress [LC-USZ62-2583]; p.64 S. E. Forman. Essentials in Civil Government, A Text-Book for Use in Schools. New York: American Book Company, 1915; p.65 Library of Congress [LC-USZ62-53337]; p.71 Library of Congress [LC-USZ62-14511]; p.72, p.118, p.149, p.154 (left) North Wind Picture Archives; p.73 A Brief History of the United States by Joel Dorman Steele and Esther Baker Steele, 1885 [Public domain], via Wikimedia Commons; p.75 Library of Congress [LC-DIG-pga-02418]; p.76, p.136, p.152, p.174 North Wind Picture Archives/Alamy; p.78 Library of Congress [LC-DIG-pga-03318]; p.79 Ivy Close Images/Alamy; p.80 Heritage Image Partnership Ltd/Alamy; p.81 Cassell's illustrated history of England, Volume 5. London, Paris, New York: Cassell Petter & Galpin; p.83 Everett Historical/ Shutterstock; p.84 (left) By Hoshie [Public domain, via Wikimedia Commons]; p.84 (right), p.109 (left) By DevinCook Created by Jacobolus [Public domain], via Wikimedia Commons; p.89 (left) Stephen Dorey-Bygone Images/Alamy; p.95 George Washington Papers, Series 4, General Correspondence: Talmadge, 1783, Codes/Library of Congress; p.98 Library of Congress [LC-DIG-highsm-02890]; p.99 Ogden, Ruth and Ogden, Henry Alexander. A Loyal Little Red-Coat: A Story of Child-Life in New York a Hundred Years Ago. New York: Frederick A. Stokes, 1900; p.100 Library of Congress [LC-USZ62-7407]; p.101 Library of Congress [LC-USZ62-10658]; p.102 National Archives and Records Administration; p.103 Art Collection 2/Alamy; p.104 USA.gov/United States Government; p.107 Library of Congress Geography and Map Division; p.108 Morris, Charles. A History of the United States of America; Its People and Its Institutions. Philadelphia and London: J. B. Lippincott Company, 1914; p.109 (right) By Dbenbenn, Zscout370, Jacobolus, Indolences, Technion. [Public domain], via Wikimedia Commons; p.110 World History Archive/Alamy; p.111 By Benjamin Franklin and David Hall (printers) (Image by Godot13) [Public domain], via Wikimedia Commons; p.113, p.114 (top) By US Mint (coin), National Numismatic Collection (photograph by Jaclyn Nash) [Public domain], via Wikimedia Commons; p.115 Library of Congress [LC-DIG-pga-02322]; p.116 (left) Library of Congress [LC-DIG-ppmsca-30581]; p.116 (center) Library of Congress [LC-DIG-pga-11392]; 118 R Library of Congress [LC-DIG-pga-13908]; p.119 (right) Edwin Verin/Alamy; p.121 Library of Congress [LC-DIG-stereo-1s05856]; p.123 Library of Congress [LC-DIG-ppmsca-35645]; p.125 (left) Montgomery, D. H. The Leading Facts of American History. Boston: Ginn and Company, 1910; p.126 Scott, David B. A School History of the United States, from the Discovery of America to the Year 1870. New York: Harper & brothers, 1870; p.127 (right) Antiqua Print Gallery/Alamy; p.129 Paul Fearn/Alamy; p.130 Library of Congress [LC-USZ62-37836]; p.131 Library of Congress [LC-USZ62-110379]; p.132 J. Kirkland and C. Kirkland. The Story of Chicago (Vol. II); p.134, p.162 (bottom) Pictorial Press Ltd/Alamy; p.135 Artokoloro Quint Lox Limited/ Alamy; p.138 Nikater/Wikimedia Commons; p.139 By Internet Archive Book Images [No restrictions], via Wikimedia Commons; p.140 Library of Congress [LC-USZC4-2946]; p.141 Library of Congress, Serial and Government Publications Division; p.142 PF-(usna)/Alamy; p.145 The National Map/U.S. Department of the Interior/U.S. Geological Survey; p.146 Library of Congress [PAN US GEOG - Ohio no. 10 (F size) [P&P]; p.147 Luketime/Wikimedia Commons; p.150 By US Federal Government [Public domain], via Wikimedia Commons; p.151 Library of Congress [LC-DIG-nclc-02504]; p.154 (right) Classic Image/Alamy; p.155 Library of Congress Geography and Map Division; p.157 (top and bottom) Granger; p.161 Stowe, Harriet Beecher. Uncle Tom's Cabin: or, Life Among the Lowly. Boston: John P. Jewett & Co.; Cleveland: Jewett, Proctor & Worthington, 1852; p.163 Library of Congress [LC-USZ62-130171]; p.165 Map from The Ox Team, or the Old Oregon Trail 1852–1906, by Ezra Meeker/University of Texas Libraries/Wikimedia Commons; p.166 Library of Congress [LC-DIG-pga-12399]; p.168 By Dlm82 at English Wikipedia [Public domain], via Wikimedia Commons; p.170 Library of Congress [LC-USZ62-58600]; p.171 Library of Congress [LC-DIG-det-4a18123]; p.172 Library of Congress [2004629238]; p.175 Library of Congress [LC-DIG-ppmsca-35361]; p.177 Everett Historical/Shutterstock; p.180 1890's caricature of Americans kicking out the British. Uncle Sam looks on as a youthful George Washington in tricorne hat kicks John Bull across the water, out of "U.S." and back to "England"/Wikimedia Commons; p.181 Montgomery, D. H. The Student's American History. Publisher: Boston and London: Ginn & Company, 1899; p.182 Library of Congress Geography and Map Division Washington, D.C. 20540-4650 dcu; p.183 (left) Library of Congress [LC-USZ62-62797]; p.183 (right) Library of Congress [LC-USZC4-2522]; p.185 Library of Congress [LC-USZ62-28860]; p.187 Universal Images Group North America LLC/Alamy; p.188 Library of Congress [LC-DIG-ppmsca-33640]; p.191 (left) Library of Congress [LC-DIG-det-4a04042]; p.191 (right) FL Historical 30/Alamy; p.194 Library of Congress [LC-USZ62-130158]; p.194 (left) Library of Congress [LC-DIG-stereo-1s02441]; p.194 (right) Library of Congress [LC-DIG-stereo-1s02802]; all other images from iStock and/or Shutterstock.

Standards

© 2014 Mid-continent Research for Education and Learning (McREL)
© 2010 National Council for the Social Studies (NCSS), The College, Career, and Civic Life (C3) Framework for Social Studies State Standards: Guidance for Enhancing the Rigor of K–12 Civics, Economics, Geography, and History

For information on how this resource meets national and other state standards, see pages 12–14. You may also review this information by visiting our website at www.teachercreatedmaterials.com/ administrators/correlations/ and following the on-screen directions.

Shell Education

A division of Teacher Created Materials
5301 Oceanus Drive
Huntington Beach, CA 92649-1030
www.tcmpub.com/shell-education

ISBN 978-1-4258-1397-0
©2018 Shell Educational Publishing, Inc.

Table of Contents

Introduction

In the complex global world of the 21st century, it is essential for citizens to have the foundational knowledge and analytic skills to understand the barrage of information surrounding them. An effective social studies program will provide students with these analytic skills and prepare them to understand and make intentional decisions about their country and the world. A well-designed social studies program develops active citizens who are able to consider multiple viewpoints and the possible consequences of various decisions.

The four disciplines of social studies enable students to understand their relationships with other people—those who are similar and those from diverse backgrounds. Students come to appreciate the foundations of the American democratic system and the importance of civic involvement. They have opportunities to understand the historic and economic forces that have resulted in the world and United States of today. They will also explore geography to better understand the nature of Earth and the effects of human interactions.

It is essential that social studies addresses more than basic knowledge. In each grade, content knowledge is a vehicle for students to engage in deep, rich thinking. They must problem solve, make decisions, work cooperatively as well as alone, make connections, and make reasoned value judgments. The world and the United States are rapidly changing. Students must be prepared for the world they will soon lead.

The Need for Practice

To be successful in today's social studies classrooms, students must understand both basic knowledge and the application of ideas to new or novel situations. They must be able to discuss and apply their ideas in coherent and rational ways. Practice is essential if they are to internalize social studies concepts, skills, and big ideas. Practice is crucial to help students have the experience and confidence to apply the critical-thinking skills needed to be active citizens in a global society.

Introduction *(cont.)*

Understanding Assessment

In addition to providing opportunities for frequent practice, teachers must be able to assess students' understanding of social studies concepts, big ideas, vocabulary, and reasoning. This is important so teachers can effectively address students' misconceptions and gaps, build on their current understanding, and challenge their thinking at an appropriate level. Assessment is a long-term process that involves careful analysis of student responses from a multitude of sources. In the social studies context, this could include classroom discussions, projects, presentations, practice sheets, or tests. When analyzing the data, it is important for teachers to reflect on how their teaching practices may have influenced students' responses and to identify those areas where additional instruction may be required. Essentially, the data gathered from assessment should be used to inform instruction: to slow down, to continue as planned, to speed up, or to reteach in a new way.

Best Practices for This Series

- Use the practice pages to introduce important social studies topics to your students.

- Use the Weekly Topics and Themes chart from pages 5–7 to align the content to what you're covering in class. Then, treat the pages in this book as jumping off points for that content.

- Use the practice pages as formative assessment of the key social studies disciplines: history, civics, geography, and economics.

- Use the weekly themes to engage students in content that is new to them.

- Encourage students to independently learn more about the topics introduced in this series.

- Challenge students with some of the more complex weeks by leading teacher-directed discussions of the vocabulary and concepts presented.

- Support students in practicing the varied types of questions asked throughout the practice pages.

- Use the texts in this book to extend your teaching of close reading, responding to text-dependent questions, and providing evidence for answers.

How to Use This Book

180 Days of Social Studies offers teachers and parents a full page of social studies practice for each day of the school year.

Weekly Structure

These activities reinforce grade-level skills across a variety of social studies concepts. The content and questions are provided as full practice pages, making them easy to prepare and implement as part of a classroom routine or for homework.

Every practice page provides content, questions, and/or tasks that are tied to a social studies topic and standard. Students are given opportunities for regular practice in social studies, allowing them to build confidence through these quick standards-based activities.

Weekly Topics and Themes

The activities are organized by a weekly topic within one of the four social studies disciplines: history, civics, geography, and economics. The following chart shows the topics that are covered during each week of instruction:

Week	Discipline	Social Studies Topic	C3 Focus
1	History	American Indians prior to European exploration	Culture; People, places, and environments
2	Civics	Know and interpret songs, symbols, Pledge of Allegiance that express American ideals	Civic ideals and practices; Culture
3	Geography	Early American Indians settlement in North America; Adaptation and use of environment	People, places, and environments
4	Economics	Economy of early American Indians	Production, distribution, and consumption
5	History	Early explorers and settlement in the western hemisphere	Time, continuity and change; Production, distribution, and consumption
6	Civics	Origins and significance of national monuments, locations and events	Civic ideals and practices; Culture
7	Geography	Geography of early explorers in the western hemisphere	People, places, and environments
8	Economics	Columbian exchange, trade with American Indians	People, places, and environments; Production, distribution, and consumption
9	History	Colonization of North America	People, places, and environments; Culture

How to Use This Book *(cont.)*

Week	Discipline	Social Studies Topic	C3 Focus
10	Civics	Colonial government	Civic ideals and practices; Power, authority, and governance
11	Geography	Settlement of the 13 colonies	People, places, and environments
12	Economics	Major industries of colonial America	Production, distribution, and consumption
13	History	Lead up to the Revolutionary War	Production, distribution, and consumption; Time, continuity and change
14	Civics	Patriots and loyalists prior to the Revolutionary War	Civic ideals and practices; Power, authority, and governance
15	Geography	Key locations in the 13 colonies; First expansion of America; Triangular trade	People, places, and environment
16	Economics	Mercantilism; British control American economy prior to the American Revolution	Production, distribution, and consumption
17	History	Revolutionary War—Significant people	Power, authority, and governance; Individuals, groups, and institutions
18	Civics	Revolutionary War—important documents	Power, authority, and governance; Civic ideals and practices
19	Geography	Important battles of the Revolutionary War	People, places, and environment
20	Economics	Economics during the Revolutionary War	Production, distribution, and consumption
21	History	Founding Fathers; Slavery after the Revolutionary War	Power, authority, and governance; Individuals, groups, and institutions
22	Civics	Powers granted to federal government and those reserved for the states The American Constitution; Civic duties; Bill of Rights	Power, authority, and governance; Civic ideals and practices
23	Geography	Slavery in the United States; Expansion of America	People, places, and environment; Production, distribution, and consumption

51397—180 Days of Social Studies

© *Shell Education*

How to Use This Book (cont.)

Week	Discipline	Social Studies Topic	C3 Focus
24	Economics	Inventions that helped America prosper and expand	Production, distribution, and consumption; People, places, and environment
25	History	War of 1812—Reasons and Consequences	Time, continuity, and change; Production, distribution, and consumption
26	Civics	National holidays, celebrations that promote citizenship and unity	Civic ideals and practices; Individuals, groups, and institutions
27	Geography	Westward expansion and exploration from 1800–1860s	People, places, and environments
28	Economics	Immigration, migration, and limited resources	People, places, and environments; Production, distribution, and consumption
29	History	Oregon Trail—Reasons and consequences	Time, continuity, and change
30	Civics	Federalism/anti-federalism factors that influenced the Civil War	Civic ideals and practices
31	Geography	Physical resources that encouraged westward expansion	People, places, and environments
32	Economics	The impact of inventions on the economy of individuals and society	Production, distribution, and consumption
33	History	Impact of 19th century and the Civil War	People, places, and environments
34	Civics	Civic duties	Civic ideals and practices
35	Geography	Impact of natural features on human actions	People, places, and environments
36	Economics	Impact of 19th-century innovations and inventions on settlement	Production, distribution, and consumption

How to Use This Book *(cont.)*

Using the Practice Pages

Practice pages provide instruction and assessment opportunities for each day of the school year. Days 1 to 4 provide content in short texts or graphics followed by related questions or tasks. Day 5 provides an application task based on the week's work.

All four social studies disciplines are practiced. There are nine weeks of topics for each discipline. The discipline is indicated on the margin of each page.

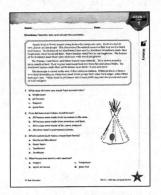

Day 1: Students read a text about the weekly topic and answer questions. This day provides a general introduction to the week's topic.

Day 2: Students read a text and answer questions. Typically, this content is more specialized than Day 1.

Day 3: Students analyze a primary source or other graphic (chart, table, graph, or infographic) related to the weekly topic and answer questions.

How to Use This Book *(cont.)*

Using the Practice Pages *(cont.)*

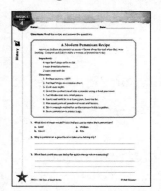

Day 4: Students analyze an image or text and answer questions. Then, students make connections to their own lives.

Day 5: Students analyze a primary source or other graphic and respond to it using knowledge they've gained throughout the week. This day serves as an application of what they've learned.

Diagnostic Assessment

Teachers can use the practice pages as diagnostic assessments. The data analysis tools included with the book enable teachers or parents to quickly score students' work and monitor their progress. Teachers and parents can see which skills students may need to target further to develop proficiency.

Students will learn skills to support informational text analysis, primary source analysis, how to make connections to self, and how to apply what they learned. To assess students' learning in these areas, check their answers based on the answer key or use the *Response Rubric* (page 212) for constructed-response questions that you want to evaluate more deeply. Then, record student scores on the *Practice Page Item Analysis* (page 213). You may also wish to complete a *Student Item Analysis by Discipline* for each student (pages 214–215). These charts are also provided in the Digital Resources as PDFs, *Microsoft Word®* files, and *Microsoft Excel®* files. Teachers can input data into the electronic files directly on the computer, or they can print the pages. See page 216 for more information.

How to Use This Book (cont.)

Diagnostic Assessment (cont.)

Practice Page Item Analyses

Every four weeks, follow these steps:

- Choose the four-week range you're assessing in the first row.

- Write or type the students' names in the far left column. Depending on the number of students, more than one copy of the form may be needed.

  - The skills are indicated across the top of the chart.

- For each student, record how many correct answers they gave and/or their rubric scores in the appropriate columns. There will be four numbers in each cell, one for each week. You can view which students are or are not understanding the social studies concepts or student progress after multiple opportunities to respond to specific text types or question forms.

- Review students' work for the first four sections. Add the scores for each student, and write that sum in the far right column. Use these scores as benchmarks to determine how each student is performing.

Student Item Analyses by Discipline

For each discipline, follow these steps:

- Write or type the student's name on the top of the charts.

  - The skills are indicated across the tops of the charts.

- Select the appropriate discipline and week.

- For each student, record how many correct answers they gave and/or their rubric scores in the appropriate columns. You can view which students are or are not understanding each social studies discipline or student progress after multiple opportunities to respond to specific text types or question forms.

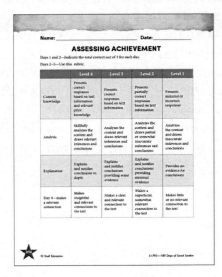

How to Use This Book *(cont.)*

Using the Results to Differentiate Instruction

Once results are gathered and analyzed, teachers can use the results to inform the way they differentiate instruction. The data can help determine which social studies skills and content are the most difficult for students and which students need additional instructional support and continued practice. Depending on how often the practice pages are scored, results can be considered for instructional support on a weekly or monthly basis.

Whole-Class Support

The results of the diagnostic analysis may show that the entire class is struggling with a particular concept or group of concepts. If these concepts have been taught in the past, this indicates that further instruction or reteaching is necessary. If these concepts have not been taught in the past, this data is a great preassessment and demonstrate that students do not have a working knowledge of the concepts. Thus, careful planning for the length of the unit(s) or lesson(s) must be considered, and extra front-loading may be required.

Small-Group or Individual Support

The results of the diagnostic analysis may show that an individual or a small group of students is struggling with a particular concept or group of concepts. If these concepts have been taught in the past, this indicates that further instruction or reteaching is necessary. Consider pulling aside these students while others are working independently to instruct further on the concept(s). You can also use the result to help identify individuals or groups of proficient students who are ready for enrichment or above-grade-level instruction. These students may benefit from independent learning contracts or more challenging activities.

Digital Resources

The Digital Resources contain PDFs and editable digital copies of the rubrics and item analysis pages. See page 216 for more information.

Standards Correlations

Shell Education is committed to producing educational materials that are research and standards based. In this effort, we have correlated all products to the academic standards of all 50 states, the District of Columbia, the Department of Defense Dependent Schools, and the Canadian provinces.

How to Find Standards Correlations

To print a customized correlation report of this product for your state, visit our website at **www.teachercreatedmaterials.com/administrators/correlations/** and follow the online directions. If you require assistance in printing correlation reports, please contact the Customer Service Department at 1-877-777-3450.

Purpose and Intent of Standards

The Every Student Succeeds Act (ESSA) mandates that all states adopt challenging academic standards that help students meet the goal of college and career readiness. While many states already adopted academic standards prior to ESSA, the act continues to hold states accountable for detailed and comprehensive standards.

Standards are designed to focus instruction and guide adoption of curricula. Standards are statements that describe the criteria necessary for students to meet specific academic goals. They define the knowledge, skills, and content students should acquire at each level. Standards are also used to develop standardized tests to evaluate students' academic progress. Teachers are required to demonstrate how their lessons meet state standards. State standards are used in the development of all of our products, so educators can be assured they meet the academic requirements of each state.

NCSS Standards and the C3 Framework

The lessons in this book are aligned to the National Council for the Social Studies (NCSS) standards and the C3 Framework. The chart on pages 5–7 lists the NCSS themes used throughout this book.

McREL Compendium

Each year, McREL analyzes state standards and revises the compendium to produce a general compilation of national standards. The chart on pages 13–14 correlates specific McREL standards to the content covered each week.

Standards Correlations *(cont.)*

Week	McREL SS Standard
1	Understands the characteristics of societies in the Americas, Western Europe, and Western Africa that increasingly interacted after 1450
2	Understands the importance of Americans sharing and supporting certain values, beliefs, and principles of American constitutional democracy
3	Understands the nature, distribution and migration of human populations on Earth's surface Understands the patterns of human settlement and their causes
4	Understands characteristics of different economic systems, economic institutions, and economic incentives
5	Understands cultural and ecological interactions among previously unconnected people resulting from early European exploration and colonization
6	Understands the importance of Americans sharing and supporting certain values, beliefs, and principles of American constitutional democracy
7	Understands the characteristics and uses of maps, globes, and other geographic tools and technologies Understands the patterns of human settlement and their causes
8	Understands characteristics of different economic systems, economic institutions, and economic incentives
9	Understands cultural and ecological interactions among previously unconnected people resulting from early European exploration and colonization Understands why the Americas attracted Europeans, why they brought enslaved Africans to their colonies and how Europeans struggled for control of North America and the Caribbean
10	Understands the relationships among liberalism, republicanism, and American constitutional democracy
11	Understands the patterns of human settlement and their causes Understands how physical systems affect human systems
12	Understands that scarcity of productive resources requires choices that generate opportunity costs
13	Understands how political, religious, and social institutions emerged in the English colonies Understands how the values and institutions of European economic life took root in the colonies and how slavery reshaped European and African life in the Americas
14	Understands the relationships among liberalism, republicanism, and American constitutional democracy
15	Understands how physical systems affect human systemsUnderstands the nature, distribution and migration of human populations on Earth's surface
16	Understands characteristics of different economic systems, economic institutions, and economic incentives
17	Understands the causes of the American Revolution, the ideas and interests involved in shaping the revolutionary movement, and reasons for the American victory Understands the impact of the American Revolution on politics, economy, and society
18	Understands the relationships among liberalism, republicanism, and American constitutional democracy Understands the importance of Americans sharing and supporting certain values, beliefs, and principles of American constitutional democracy

Standards Correlations *(cont.)*

Week	McREL SS Standard
19	Understands How Physical Systems Affect Human Systems Understands the patterns of human settlement and their causes
20	Understands characteristics of different economic systems, economic institutions, and economic incentives
21	Understands the institutions and practices of government created during the Revolution and how these elements were revised between 1787 and 1815 to create the foundation of the American political system based on the U.S. Constitution and the Bill of Rights Understands the impact of the American Revolution on politics, economy, and society
22	Understands how the United States Constitution grants and distributes power and responsibilities to national and state government and how it seeks to prevent the abuse of power Understands issues concerning the relationship between state and local governments and the national government and issues pertaining to representation at all three levels of government
23	Understands the patterns and networks of economic interdependence on Earth's surface Understands the patterns of human settlement and their causes
24	Understands that scarcity of productive resources requires choices that generate opportunity costs
25	Understands the United States territorial expansion between 1801 and 1861, and how it affected relations with external powers and American Indians Understands how the industrial revolution, increasing immigration, the rapid expansion of slavery, and the westward movement changed American lives and led to regional tensions
26	Understands the importance of Americans sharing and supporting certain values, beliefs, and principles of American constitutional democracy
27	Understands the patterns of human settlement and their causes
28	Understands that scarcity of productive resources requires choices that generate opportunity costs
29	Understands how the industrial revolution, increasing immigration, the rapid expansion of slavery, and the westward movement changed American lives and led to regional tensions Understands the extension, restriction, and reorganization of political democracy after 1800
30	Understands the relationships among liberalism, republicanism, and American constitutional democracy
31	Understands the patterns of human settlement and their causes
32	Understands that scarcity of productive resources requires choices that generate opportunity costs
33	Understands the course and character of the Civil War and its effects on the American people Understands the causes of the Civil War
34	Understands how certain character traits enhance citizens' ability to fulfill personal and civic responsibilities Understands how participation in civic and political life can help citizens attain individual and public goals
35	Understands how physical systems affect human systems
36	Understands that scarcity of productive resources requires choices that generate opportunity costs

Name: _____ **Date:** _____

Directions: Read the text, and answer the questions.

History

> People lived in North America long before the Europeans came. Each area had its own climate and landscape. This determined the natural resources that they used to build their homes. The American Indians of the Northwest Coast and the Northeast Woodlands made their longhouses out of wood and bark. These buildings were best in cold weather. Many families would live in one longhouse. The American Indians of the Southeast made their open-air houses with wood and grasses.
>
> The Plateau, Great Basin, and Plains Indians were nomadic. They moved around a lot in search of food. Their tepees were made from tree branches and animal hides. The Southwest Indians made their adobe homes from bricks of clay and straw.
>
> The landscape is varied in the area of the California Indians. Different kinds of homes were built depending on where they lived. Some groups built cedar bark lodges, while others built grass huts. Others lived in pit houses, which were partly dug into the ground and made of mud and grass.

1. What type of home was made from animal hides?
   a. longhouses
   b. pit houses
   c. tepees
   d. grass huts

2. How did American Indians build homes?
   a. All homes were made from resources in the area.
   b. All homes were made from branches and bark.
   c. All houses were made of the same material.
   d. All tribes lived in permanent homes.

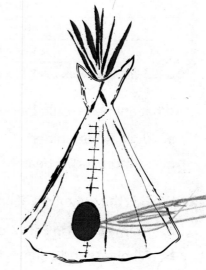

3. Which culture built homes made from bricks?
   a. Northeast Woodland
   b. Great Basin
   c. Southwest
   d. Southeast

4. What house was best in cold weather?
   a. tepee
   b. open-air house
   c. longhouse
   d. grass hut

History

Name: _____ Date: _____

Directions: Review the chart, and answer the questions.

The Human Traits of Animals	
Animal	**Its Totem Pole Meaning**
bear	courage
beaver	strong will
bison	great strength
coyote	smart trickster
deer	survival
dog	loyalty
eagle	freedom
fox	observation
raccoon	curiosity
porcupine	trust
salmon	determination
squirrel	planning
snake	healing
spider	creativity
turtle	Mother Earth
wolf	leadership

American Indians believe that plants and animals have souls. This belief is called *animism*. Some tribes believe that animals have human traits. The Northwest Indians carve animals on totem poles. The carved animals show the human traits of a family.

1. What animals would be on a totem pole that means Mother Earth, loyalty, and creativity?

    a. deer, turtle, spider   **c.** turtle, dog, spider

    b. salmon, turtle, bear   **d.** turtle, buffalo, wolf

2. What is the definition of *animism*?

    a. Animals are on Earth for people to use.   **c.** Dogs are not loyal to people.

    b. All plants and animals have souls.   **d.** Spiders weave stories about American Indians.

3. You have been asked to help design your family's totem pole. What animals would you carve on the pole? Why?

    _____

    _____

    _____

Name:_____ Date:_____

Directions: Review the chart, and answer the questions.

Foods of American Indian Cultures			
American Indian Group	**Method**	**Types of Food**	**Observations**
Northwest	hunting, gathering, fishing	wild plants, fish, small animals	lots of food available
Northeast Woodland	hunting, gathering, farming	deer, fox, small animals, corn, beans, and squash	used spears, bows and arrows to hunt
Southeast	hunting, gathering, fishing, farming	small animals, birds, melons, peaches, tobacco	growing season year round
Plains	hunting, gathering, farming	bison, moose, elk, lynx, corn, beans, and squash	used "buffalo jumps" to hunt
California	hunting, gathering, fishing	fish, seaweed, acorns, seeds, berries, wild plants	plentiful food, growing season year round
Plateau	hunting, gathering, fishing	fish, eels, deer, elk, bear, caribou, berries, wild plants	used spears, bows and arrows to hunt
Great Basin	hunting, gathering	small animals, birds, seeds, roots, cacti, insects	nomadic due to their need to search for food
Southwest	hunting, gathering, farming	small animals, birds, nuts, berries, corn, beans, and squash	farmed if near water

1. What culture was nomadic?

   a. Northeast

   b. California

   c. Great Basin

   d. Southeast

2. Which culture hunted with "buffalo jumps"?

   a. Plains

   b. Plateau

   c. Northeast

   d. Southwest

3. What kind of food did the hunters and gatherers eat?

   _____

   _____

Geography

Geography

Name: _____ **Date:** _____

Directions: Look at the pictures, and answer the questions.

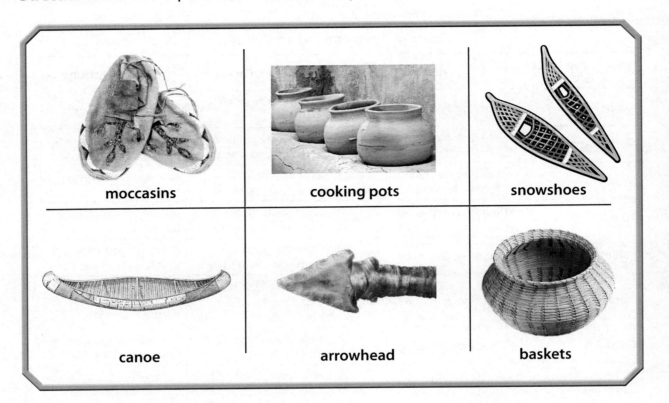

moccasins	cooking pots	snowshoes
canoe	arrowhead	baskets

1. What do all the items have in common?

   a. All items are used only by women.   **c.** All items are for hunting.

   b. All items are made with natural materials.   **d.** All items are used to make food.

2. Choose one artifact shown above. Explain what it is made from, what it is used for, and who would use it.

   _____

   _____

   _____

3. Choose one of the artifacts. What material is it made from today, and who uses it?

   _____

   _____

   _____

Name: _____ **Date:** _____

Directions: Read the text, and answer the questions.

North American Indians were excellent farmers. They planted the "Three Sisters" —corn, beans, squash—together in a way that helped each of them grow. This is called "companion planting." The roots of the beans put nitrogen into the soil, which fed the corn. The corn acted as a pole for the beans. The squash leaves shaded the ground to keep the soil moist.

The beans and corn were left to age and dry. This increased the amount of protein in the food. The "Three Sisters" together provided a lot of the food needs of the American Indian.

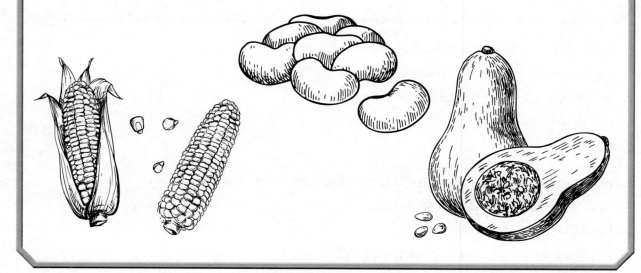

1. What were the benefits of planting corn, beans, and squash together?

   _____

   _____

   _____

   _____

2. What is a dish you eat made with one of these plants?

   _____

   _____

   _____

Economics

Name: _____ **Date:** _____

Directions: Read the text, and answer the questions.

The early American Indians relied on natural resources to meet basic needs. Men made weapons to kill animals for food and clothing. They made tools to trap animals and fish. Canoes were made from wood for travel. Women made pots from clay, stone, or wood. They gathered food and wove baskets from reeds and strips of plants. The trading of seeds brought agriculture to most American Indian cultures. The "Three Sisters" (corn, beans, and squash) became common crops. Trade centers developed near travel routes on lakes and rivers. They traded extra resources as part of their local economies. Some tribes used beads made of shells or stone as a form of money to trade for items they needed.

1. What did men do to support their tribe's economy?
   a. They wove reeds into baskets.
   b. They made clothes out of animal hides.
   c. They gathered seeds.
   d. They hunted animals.

2. How did the early American Indians use their environments to survive?
   a. They were hunters and gatherers.
   b. All tribes were farmers.
   c. They used iron pots to cook their food.
   d. American Indians ate only plants.

3. Which one of the following was NOT part of the economy of the early American Indians?
   a. trading extra goods for things they needed
   b. hunting and gathering food
   c. doing jobs for payment
   d. storing food for later use

4. How did trading help American Indians produce more food?
   a. Tribes traded seeds.
   b. Tribes traded gardening tools.
   c. Tribes traded plants.
   d. Tribes traded containers to save seeds.

Name: _____ Date: _____

Directions: Review the timeline, and answer the questions.

Developments in North America, 200–1620

| AD 200–1000 | AD 1142 | | AD 1565 | AD 1607 | AD 1620 |

Farming spreads among American Indians.

Iroquois League creates constitution.

Spain founds St. Augustine, Florida.

Britain founds Jamestown, Virginia.

Puritans land at Plymouth Rock, Massachusetts.

Economics

1. When did American Indians start farming?

   a. AD 1565

   b. AD 1607

   c. AD 200

   d. AD 1142

2. Based on the information provided by this timeline, which statement is true?

   a. Jamestown was founded before St. Augustine.

   b. Spain founds St. Augustine.

   c. Farming spreads after the Iroquois Constitution is made.

   d. The Puritans arrived in Plymouth before the Spanish in Florida.

3. What do you think are the two most important dates for American Indians on this timeline? Why?

   _____

   _____

   _____

   _____

   _____

   _____

   _____

Name: _____ Date: _____

Directions: Review the map, and answer the questions.

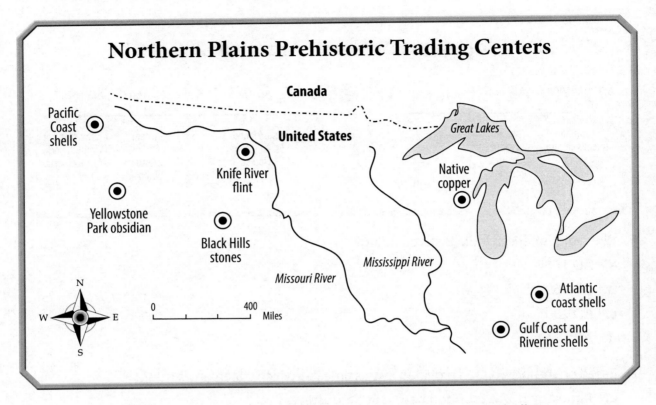

Northern Plains Prehistoric Trading Centers

1. What direction did traders travel from Knife River to get Pacific Coast shells?

   a. west

   b. northeast

   c. southwest

   d. north

2. Where would American Indians get their copper?

   a. from the Pacific Coast trading center

   b. from the Black Hills trading center

   c. from the trading center near the Great Lakes

   d. from the Atlantic Coast trading center

3. How many miles would traders have to travel from Yellowstone Park trading center to Knife River trading center?

   a. 50 miles

   b. 10 miles

   c. 350 miles

   d. 600 miles

Name: _____ **Date:** _____

Directions: Study the picture, and answer the questions.

Economics

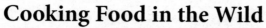
Cooking Food in the Wild

1. American Indians ate food caught in the wild. Based on the image, how did they prepare their food?

   a. They cooked using natural gas.

   b. They cooked on a wood fire.

   c. They cooked on a barbecue.

   d. They served their food raw.

2. How would you prepare food outside?

   _____

   _____

   _____

3. What kind of food does your family cook outside?

   _____

   _____

   _____

Economics

Name:_____ Date:_____

Directions: Study the picture, and answer the question.

Hunting, Gathering, and Farming

1. This picture was drawn by an American Indian youth. Explain how it shows that people in his culture were hunters, gatherers, and farmers.

_____

_____

_____

_____

_____

_____

_____

51397—180 Days of Social Studies

© *Shell Education*

Name: _____ **Date:** _____

History

Directions: Read the text, and answer the questions.

The 1400s were the beginning of the European Age of Discovery. People wanted spices from Asia to flavor food and preserve their meat. Explorers from all over Europe sailed to the west to find a faster route to Asia. They found an entire continent in the way—North America. For the next 200 years, North America was explored and mapped.

The captains of the ships needed people who could do different jobs. Sailors were needed to work the sails. Navigators were needed to guide the ships. Priests recorded trip information in journals. Soldiers were needed for protection when they reached shore.

1. What were spices used for in the Age of Discovery?
   a. to color food
   b. for money
   c. for ink to write with
   d. to preserve meat

2. During the Age of Discovery, where were the explorers from?
   a. China
   b. North America
   c. Europe
   d. Africa

3. What was the job of a priest on board a ship?
   a. record their travels
   b. feed the sailors
   c. give protection
   d. do the navigation

4. What did the explorers find instead of a route to Asia?
   a. gold
   b. a continent
   c. spices
   d. a large river

History

Name:_____ Date:_____

Directions: Review the timeline, and answer the questions.

European Explorers

1492	1513	1539–41	1565	1585 & 1587	1607
Christopher Columbus, an Italian explorer, claimed land in the Western Hemisphere for Spain.	Juan Ponce de León, a Spanish explorer, claimed Florida for Spain.	Hernando de Soto, from Spain, explored from Florida to Louisiana to Tennessee.	Pedro Menéndez de Avilés founded St. Augustine, Florida, for Spain—the first permanent settlement in America.	Sir Walter Raleigh sent settlers from Britain. They founded Roanoke Colony, but it did not survive.	Britain sponsored the first permanent British colony in Jamestown.

1. Which European explorer was the first to claim land in the Western Hemisphere?

    a. Pedro Menéndez de Avilés

    b. Christopher Columbus

    c. Hernando de Soto

    d. Juan Ponce de León

2. Where was the first permanent British colony?

    a. Jamestown

    b. Plymouth

    c. St. Augustine

    d. New York

3. Where was the first permanent settlement in the United States?

    a. Florida

    b. New York

    c. Roanoke

    d. Jamestown

4. Who was the first Spanish explorer to claim part of North America?

    a. Pedro Menéndez de Avilés

    b. Juan Ponce de León

    c. Hernando de Soto

    d. Christopher Columbus

Name: _____ **Date:** _____

Directions: Study the picture, and answer the questions.

1. What did the American Indians give the Europeans in trade?

   a. tobacco

   b. cloth

   c. furs

   d. barrels

2. What did the American Indians use to hunt animals?

   a. guns

   b. bows and arrows

   c. snares

   d. hatchets

3. Use the chart to compare what the Europeans and the American Indians wore.

European Clothing	Both	American Indian Clothing

History

Name: _____ Date: _____

Directions: Read the text, and answer the questions.

> Explorers from Spain, Portugal, France, Britain, Netherlands, and Italy risked their lives to find a new way to Asia. They all had their own reasons to head out across the ocean.
>
> | **Gold** | **God** | **Glory** |
> |---|---|---|
> | Explorers wanted to bring back silk, spices, and gold for their king or queen. All these things were very valuable. When they brought back treasures from their travels, they were rewarded with gold. | Some explorers traveled to spread their Christian beliefs to the people that they found in the New World. God's blessing would be their reward. | Explorers claimed land for their country on their trips west. They craved the praise that they received from their king or queen when they returned home. The explorers were proud of having places named after them in the New World. |

1. How were the explorers paid for their work? Circle all that apply.

   a. rewards from God

   b. the honor of having a place named after them

   c. gold and praise from the king or queen

   d. all the above

2. Explorers claimed land for their country. What did they get in return?

   a. God's blessing

   b. praise from the king or queen

   c. reward of gold and silver

   d. silk and spices

3. You have been asked by the king to be his explorer to the New World. What would motivate you to explore: gold, God, or glory? Explain your choice.

   _____

   _____

   _____

   _____

Name: _____ **Date:** _____

Directions: Look at the image, and answer the question.

Columbus Lands

Columbus lands in 1492.

1. View the picture through the eyes of the explorers OR through the eyes of the American Indians who already lived there. Explain how you feel and what you want to happen with the meeting. Do you think it will end well for you? Why or why not?

_____

_____

_____

_____

_____

_____

_____

Civics

Name: _____ Date: _____

Directions: Read the text, and answer the questions.

Americans are proud of their land. The United States has many interesting physical features. The National Park Service protects parks and monuments across the country. The parks are chosen for their natural beauty. Visitors enjoy outdoor activities in these parks. Some people come to hike, camp, and fish. Yellowstone was the first national park selected. People come to see hot springs, mud pots, and geysers in the park.

National monuments can be human-made or physical structures. Some examples are the Statue of Liberty and the Pullman National Monument in Chicago. Devils Tower in Wyoming was named the first national monument. It is also a sacred place for the Northern Plains Indians.

Devils Tower, Wyoming

1. Based on the text, why are national parks chosen?
    a. for historic importance
    b. for natural beauty
    c. for pride in human-made places
    d. for being the highest mountains

2. Why is Yellowstone an important national park?
    a. It receives the most visitors each year.
    b. It was the first national park.
    c. You can camp in the park all year.
    d. It has only one physical feature.

3. What is Devils Tower?
    a. a good place to go fishing
    b. a human-made structure
    c. an easy-to-climb structure
    d. the first national monument

Name: _____ Date: _____

Directions: Read the text, and answer the questions.

The faces of George Washington, Thomas Jefferson, Theodore Roosevelt, and Abraham Lincoln are carved into Mount Rushmore. Fifty-six flags fly along the Avenue of Flags at Mount Rushmore. They represent the 50 states, one district, three territories, and two commonwealths of the United States.

1. What U.S. presidents are carved into Mount Rushmore?
   a. George Washington, Thomas Jefferson, Franklin Delano Roosevelt, Abraham Lincoln
   b. George Washington, Thomas Jefferson, William McKinley, Abraham Lincoln
   c. George Washington, Andrew Jackson, Franklin Delano Roosevelt, Abraham Lincoln
   d. George Washington, Thomas Jefferson, Theodore Roosevelt, Abraham Lincoln

2. What do the flags that fly along the Avenue represent?
   a. the presidents of the United States
   b. each state, district, territory, and commonwealth of the United States
   c. the armed forces of the United States
   d. different American Indian tribes

3. Which president was chosen because he was the first president of the United States?
   a. Lincoln
   b. Roosevelt
   c. Washington
   d. Jefferson

4. If you were to carve one more face into Mount Rushmore, who would it be and why?

   _____

   _____

   _____

Civics

Name: _____ **Date:** _____

Directions: Look at the images, and answer the questions.

Fort McHenry

The British attacked Fort McHenry during the War of 1812.

1. Based on the image, which statements are correct. Circle all that apply.

   a. The soldiers are not fighting.

   b. Families can walk in the yard.

   c. The British flag flies over the fort.

   d. The ships are firing on the fort.

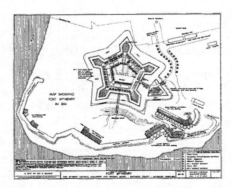

2. Study the image above. Why is a star a good shape for a fort?

   _____

   _____

   _____

Name:_____ **Date:**_____

Directions: Read the text, and answer the questions.

> This statue is on Liberty Island. It was a gift from France in 1886. The statue has many symbols important to the United States.
>
> - It sits in New York Harbor.
>
> - The crown has seven rays that represent seven seas and continents.
>
> - The torch lights the way to freedom.
>
> - The figure holds a tablet with "July 4, 1776" written on it.
>
> - The broken chains at her feet represent freedom.

1. Based on the text, which parts of the Statue of Liberty represent freedom? Circle all that apply.

   a. the seven rays

   b. the torch

   c. the tablet

   d. the chains

2. Many immigrants came to America. The Statue of Liberty was the first thing they saw. Why was this a welcoming sight for them?

   _____

   _____

   _____

   _____

3. The United States and France both had revolutions in their countries. France gave the Statue of Liberty to the United States. On another sheet of paper, write a thank you letter for the statue to the president of France.

Civics

Name: _____ Date:_____

Directions: Read the chart , and answer the question.

U.S. Landmarks		
Landmark	**Location**	**Importance**
Statue of Liberty	New York, NY	symbol of freedom and democracy
Hoover Dam	Near Boulder City, NV	symbol of scientific and industrial strength
Freedom Trail	Boston, MA	following the footsteps of U.S. forefathers
Gateway Arch	St. Louis, MO	symbol of the gateway to the West
Independence Hall	Philadelphia, PA	building where the Declaration of Independence and the U.S. Constitution were signed
Golden Gate Bridge	San Francisco, CA	a marvel of modern engineering
Mount Rushmore	Keystone, SD	represents birth, growth, development, and preservation of the United States
The Alamo	San Antonio, TX	monument of a key battle in the fight for Texas independence from Mexico
The National Mall	Washington, D.C.	collection of national buildings: White House, Washington Monument, Lincoln Memorial, World War II Memorial, Vietnam Memorial, and Smithsonian Institution
Fort Sumter	Charleston, SC	where the first shots of the Civil War were fired

1. Your family is planning a trip to see a U.S. landmark. From the chart, choose a place to go. Explain why you want to visit there.

_____

_____

_____

_____

_____

_____

_____

51397—180 Days of Social Studies

© *Shell Education*

Name: _____ **Date:** _____

Directions: Read the text, and answer the questions.

European countries claimed parts of North America in the 1600s. The American Indians met the Europeans when they first arrived. The explorers realized that the American Indians could teach them how to live off the land. The American Indians showed them the plants they ate and the animals they hunted.

The Europeans were very interested in the animal furs. There were not many furs in their home countries. Fur fashion was very popular. These fur traders quickly set up trade with the American Indian tribes in their areas. The American Indians supplied Europeans with furs. The American Indians would get guns, cloth, blankets, metal pots, and tools in return. Eventually, there was so much hunting done that there were fewer and fewer furs to trade.

1. How did the American Indians help the Europeans?
   a. They helped them to come ashore.
   b. They taught them to live off the land.
   c. They showed them how to wear furs.
   d. They traded with them for metal pots.

2. Why did American Indians trade with Europeans?
   a. to get cooking tools, blankets, and guns
   b. to get European clothing
   c. to welcome visitors to their lands
   d. to rid their land of wild animals

3. Why were the Europeans so interested in getting furs from the American Indians?
   a. They needed to learn how to hunt for furs.
   b. They had never seen furs before.
   c. There were not many furs in Europe.
   d. They wanted to learn how to use furs.

Name: _____ Date: _____

Geography

Directions: Study the map, and answer the questions.

Exploring a New Continent

Key
British - - - - ▶
Spanish ——▶

1. Where did the Spanish do most of their exploration?
   a. the southern part of North America
   b. the north Atlantic Ocean
   c. Great Lakes, Mississippi, and Atlantic coast
   d. along the Pacific coast and throughout Mexico

2. Who did the most exploration in the New World?
   a. the French
   b. the British
   c. the Dutch
   d. the Spanish

3. What direction did the explorers take to get to the New World?
   a. north
   b. east
   c. west
   d. south

51397—180 Days of Social Studies

© *Shell Education*

Name: _____ **Date:** _____

Directions: Look at the images, and read the text. Answer the questions.

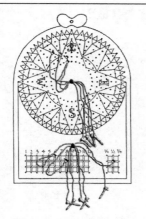

Sailors used a quadrant to measure the angle of the sun or stars. This helped them find the right direction.

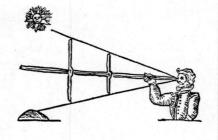

The cross-staff was used to find latitude.

Sailors used the traverse board to record travel every four hours. They recorded distance and speed.

Sailors used maps and charts to record their trips. This helped them to navigate.

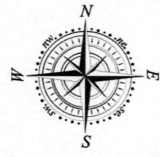

A compass rose is a figure on a map, chart, or compass. It shows what direction you are moving in or what direction something is on a map.

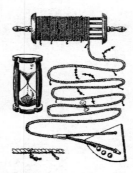

The chip log measured the speed of the ship in knots (1 knot = 1.15 miles per hour).

1. What did the chip log show?

  a. position of latitude   **c.** altitude of the sun

  b. speed of the ship   **d.** direction of the ship

2. What two navigational tools were used to record trip information?

  a. the compass rose and the chip log   **c.** the map and the traverse board

  b. the traverse board and the chip log   **d.** the cross staff and the quadrant

3. What skills would the ship's navigator need to use these tools?

_____

_____

Name: _____ **Date:** _____

Geography

Directions: Look at the map, and answer the questions.

The Expeditions of René-Robert de La Salle

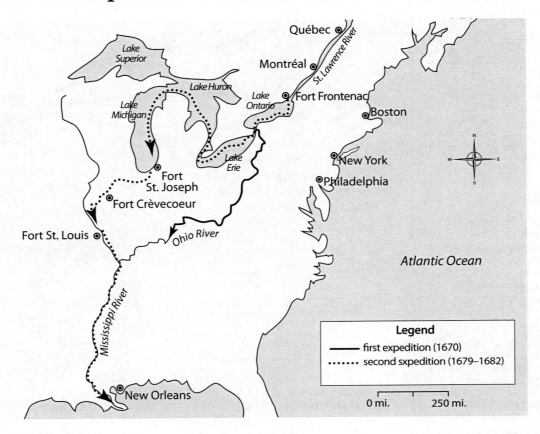

1. Using the scale and the legend, about how far did René-Robert de La Salle travel in his first expedition?

   a. 400 miles

   b. 750 miles

   c. 200 miles

   d. 1,200 miles

2. Where did the second expedition start and end?

   a. Fort Niagara and New Orleans

   b. Fort Frontenac and Fort Crèvecoeur

   c. Fort Frontenac and New Orleans

   d. Fort St. Louis and New Orleans

3. What are all the ways that you could travel from Fort St. Joseph to New Orleans today?

   _____

   _____

   _____

Name: _____ **Date:** _____

Directions: Study the image, and answer the questions.

Geography

New Homeland

1. This family has settled into their new homeland. Why would this be a good place to build a home and raise a family?

_____

_____

_____

_____

_____

_____

_____

Economics

Name: _____ **Date:** _____

Directions: Read the text, and answer the questions.

> Christopher Columbus arrived in the New World in 1492. He brought plants and animals with him. They were needed for food on his trip. The Europeans brought diseases to America without knowing it. The American Indians could not fight off these diseases. As a result, whole tribes died.
>
> The explorers traveled back to their home country to report to their king what they had found. They brought back many new plants from the New World. These new plants were planted in Europe and Africa. They also brought American Indians back with them. The Europeans enslaved the American Indians. This movement of plants, animals, people, and diseases is known as the "Columbian Exchange."

Columbus arriving in the New World

1. What is the movement of plants, animals, people, and diseases called?

   a. European trade
   b. New World Exchange
   c. American trade
   d. Columbian Exchange

2. What caused most American Indian deaths?

   a. tobacco
   b. disease
   c. guns
   d. iron weapons

3. What happened to the American Indians in Europe?

   a. became sailors
   b. became settlers
   c. became enslaved
   d. became explorers

Name: _____ **Date:** _____

Directions: Read the text, and answer the questions.

Plants were traded around the world. Europeans came to America. They took potatoes and corn to Europe. The new food made the population grow in Europe. Europeans came to America as new settlers. Cassava grew in the Caribbean. Explorers took it to Africa. It helped feed the African people. The African population grew. Coffee and cotton were new crops in America. They came from Africa and Asia.

The Europeans brought many of these new plants to America. They needed more people to work on the farms. The Europeans enslaved Africans and brought them to America. Many of these enslaved people worked on the farms.

cassava plants

Economics

1. What plants did the explorers bring back to Europe?

   a. wheat and corn

   b. potatoes and corn

   c. corn and sugarcane

   d. cassava and potatoes

2. What plants did the European explorers bring to America?

   a. cotton and coffee

   b. cassava and corn

   c. potatoes and cotton

   d. sugarcane and corn

3. What did the Europeans do to the people from Africa?

   a. brought them to work in the factories

   b. used them as sailors on their ships

   c. had them farm the new crops in Europe

   d. enslaved them

Economics

Name: _____ **Date:** _____

Directions: Look at the map, and answer the questions.

The Columbian Exchange

New World   Old World

North America

Pineapples Tomatoes Corn Avocados

Beans

Potatoes Peanuts Cassava

Turkeys

Pumpkins

Tobacco

Sugarcane Coffee

Bananas

Europe

Asia

Pears Peaches Citrus Fruits Grains • wheat • rice • barley • oats

Livestock • cattle • sheep • pig • horse

Diseases

Africa

South America

1. What were some of the things that the Old World got from the New World?

    a. tobacco, potatoes, sugarcane   **c.** pumpkins, turkeys, peaches

    b. beans, corn, pumpkins   **d.** pineapples, avocados, bananas

2. Which fruits did the New World get from the Old World?

    a. peaches, pears, bananas

    b. citrus fruit, bananas, pineapples

    c. pears, bananas, tomatoes

    d. peaches, pears, watermelons

3. What were the grains and livestock the New World got from the Old World?

    _____

    _____

    _____

51397—180 Days of Social Studies   © *Shell Education*

Name: _____ **Date:** _____

Directions: Read the graphic, and answer the questions.

The Columbian Exchange

New World

Food: corn, potatoes, beans, cocoa beans, tomatoes

Livestock: turkeys

Other: tobacco

Old World

Food: wheat, sugarcane, rice, citrus fruit, coffee beans, peaches

Livestock: horses, cows, pigs, sheep

Diseases: smallpox, measles, influenza, typhus

1. Which animals from the Old World did the American Indians use to help with their travel?

   a. cows

   b. pigs

   c. horses

   d. sheep

2. What item from the Old World are you glad came to America? Why?

   _____

   _____

   _____

3. Describe the worst thing that happened because of the Columbian Exchange.

   _____

   _____

   _____

   _____

Economics

Name: _____ **Date:** _____

Directions: Look at the images, and answer the question.

Eastern and Western Hemispheres

Eastern Hemisphere   *Western Hemisphere*

1. Choose a hemisphere. Describe how the Columbian Exchange changed the lives of the people there.

_____

_____

_____

_____

_____

_____

_____

_____

Name: _____ **Date:** _____

Directions: Read the text, and answer the questions.

Spanish, British, French, Dutch, Swedish, and German people settled along the Atlantic coast. There were many resources near the water. People in the northern colonies traded lumber, fish, whale products, and fur. People in the middle colonies traded coal, wheat, and beef. They also built ships. Cotton, rice, tobacco, and indigo (dye) were grown for trade in the South.

Some people chose to come to America as servants. They worked for no money for a set period of time. After that, they were free to do as they wished. People were also brought to America as slaves. They worked on large farms, called *plantations*, in the South.

an early map of Massachusetts

History

1. What was one of the things the settlers traded in the South?
   a. lumber
   b. fish
   c. wheat
   d. tobacco

2. Why did settlers decide to live along the Atlantic coast?
   a. People did not have a way to travel inland.
   b. The water and the land nearby had many resources.
   c. People lacked maps to find other places to settle.
   d. Their rulers in Europe told them where to settle.

3. Why were people brought to America as slaves?
   a. to work in the forests chopping trees
   b. to work in the coal mines
   c. to work on the plantations
   d. to work on the whaling ships

History

Name:_____ Date:_____

Directions: Read the text , and answer the questions.

Puritan beliefs were not allowed in Britain. So they left to find religious freedom. Religious freedom means that people can choose what to believe. A group called Pilgrims sailed to North America. They landed in November 1620. They wanted to govern themselves. The agreement was called the Mayflower Compact.

The Pilgrims had a hard winter. They had little to eat. They were very cold. A disease killed half of them. Miles Standish and William Bradford then found a good place to build the colony. It was in Plymouth, Massachusetts. The colony soon chose a governor.

replica of the Mayflower, *Boston Harbor*

1. Based on the text, why did the Pilgrims leave Britain?
   a. to find land to build their homes
   b. to find religious freedom
   c. to explore the New World
   d. to trade with their homeland

2. Based on the text, why did the Pilgrims have such a hard first year in North America?
   a. They did not know how to govern themselves.
   b. They could not find a place to build their settlement.
   c. They had little food and faced a deadly disease.
   d. They did not have a governor.

3. Based on the text, what is meant by the term *religious freedom*?
   a. People can choose what to believe.
   b. People are free to attend church or not.
   c. People can safely practice their faith in public.
   d. People practice the same faith as their leaders.

Name:_____ Date:_____

Directions: Read the chart, and answer the questions.

What the Wampanoag Taught the Pilgrims			
Food	**Clothing**	**Medicine**	**Travel**
• how to plant corn, beans, and squash • how to fertilize gardens with fish • how to grind corn into flour • how to gather safe berries to eat • how to save seeds for the next year's planting • where to fish	• what animals to hunt for hides • how to tan animal skins to make clothes	• how to gather sap from maple trees • how to use certain plants as medicine	• how to use a canoe • where the trails were

1. Based on the text, what did the Wampanoag teach the Pilgrims about medicine?

   a. how to tan animal skins

   b. how to use plants for medicine

   c. how to gather safe berries to eat

   d. where to fish

2. What did the Wampanoag NOT teach the Pilgrims?

   a. to tan hides for clothes

   b. to hunt and farm in New England

   c. to forage for berries in the woods

   d. to build houses for their settlement

3. Would the Pilgrims have survived without the help of the Wampanoag? Explain.

   _____

   _____

   _____

   _____

History

Name: _____ **Date:** _____

Directions: Study the picture, and answer the questions.

The Pilgrim Landing

1. Based on the image, what was one of the first things Pilgrim women did when the *Mayflower* landed?

   a. They washed their clothing.

   b. They helped unload the ship.

   c. They went swimming.

   d. They picked cranberries.

2. What work are male and female Pilgrims doing?

Men's Jobs	Women's Jobs

3. What jobs do people do in your family?

   _____

   _____

   _____

Name: _____ **Date:** _____

Directions: Read the text, and study the image. Answer the question.

There were 102 people on the *Mayflower* when the ship arrived in the New World in 1620. Before they even stepped onto the land, 41 of them signed an agreement. It was about how to govern the new settlement. They decided on a set of laws to follow. They also agreed that, from time to time, they would update these laws. This agreement was the Mayflower Compact.

signing the Mayflower Compact

1. Look closely at the image. What do you think shows that the Mayflower Compact was important to the Pilgrims?

_____

_____

_____

_____

_____

_____

_____

_____

_____

_____

_____

Civics

Name: _____ **Date:** _____

Directions: Read the text, and answer the questions.

The king of Britain decided who could settle in America. There were three types of colonies: royal colonies, king's friends' colonies, and charter colonies. In the first type of colony, the king owned the colony. He appointed the governor. The governor did what the king told him to do and appointed the Council.

In the second type of colony, the king gave his friends large areas of land. The landowners chose the governor and the Council. The governor would do as the king said.

In the third type of colony, the king gave charters, or grants, to companies. Each company chose its own governor and Council. Charter colonies ran their own governments. They did not report to the king, but the king could take them over at any time.

John Winthrop was a governor of the Massachusetts Bay Colony.

1. How were all colonies started?
   a. by religious groups
   b. by American Indians
   c. by the king
   d. all the above

2. Who chose the Council in charter colonies?
   a. landowners
   b. the king
   c. the governors
   d. companies

3. How might you benefit from being a friend of the king? Circle all that apply.
   a. You could be appointed as a governor.
   b. You could be elected by settlers.
   c. You could be given land.
   d. You did not have to listen to the king.

Name: _____ **Date:** _____

Directions: Read the text, and answer the questions.

Jamestown was the first permanent British settlement in America. It was settled in 1607. In Virginia, men who owned land elected people to speak for them at an assembly. The elected assembly was the first in North America. It was called the "House of Burgesses." Burgesses met yearly to solve common problems and pass laws. Famous burgesses were Patrick Henry, George Washington, and Thomas Jefferson.

Success with tobacco created problems in the colony. John Rolfe brought the crop to the area. Farmers then brought enslaved people to work in the fields. Selling tobacco made lots of money. The king wanted some of the money. He made Virginia a royal colony. He raised taxes. That made the colonists unhappy. The burgesses wanted to break away from Britain.

Patrick Henry

Civics

1. What was Virginia the first to do?
   a. become a royal colony
   b. elect an assembly
   c. get full government control
   d. break away from Britain

2. Why did the king make Virginia a royal colony?
   a. He wanted tax money from tobacco.
   b. He liked the colony's desire to set firsts.
   c. He needed a ready source of tobacco.
   d. He thought it was a way to honor the colony.

3. What did burgesses do?
   a. met yearly
   b. solved common problems
   c. passed laws
   d. all the above

Name: _____ Date: _____

Civics

Directions: Look at the graphic, and answer the questions.

How Colonial Government Worked

King of Britain: Owned the land. Approved laws.

Parliament: House of Lords was appointed by the king. Set taxes and trade rules for colonies.

Parliament: House of Commons is the elected part of government, mostly made up of wealthy men.

Colonial Governor: Appointed by the king to rule the colony. He reported directly to the king.

Council: Appointed by the governor. They made laws for the colonies. They collected taxes for the king.

Assemblies: Elected by white male landowners in the colony. Represented the citizens of each colony. Created self-government and documents to organize it.

Town Hall Meetings: Colonists met to talk about taxes, budgets, and laws.

1. Who had the most power in the 13 American colonies?

    a. the governor   **c.** the king

    b. the Assembly   **d.** the Council

2. Who was elected in the colonies?

    a. the Assembly

    b. the Council

    c. the House of Lords

    d. the House of Commons

3. What was the purpose of town hall meetings?

    _____

    _____

    _____

Name: _____ **Date:** _____

Directions: Read the text, and answer the questions.

William Penn was a Quaker. This is a Christian. Penn thought that people should be able to follow any faith. He also believed that they should have political freedom.

To help make this possible, Penn founded Philadelphia in 1682. King Charles II had given him much of what is now Pennsylvania and Delaware. Penn made agreements with local American Indians for fair use of the land.

Penn's treaty with the Indians

1. What faith did William Penn want everyone to follow?

   a. They were all to be Anglican.

   b. They all were to be Quakers.

   c. They were all to be Roman Catholic.

   d. They could follow any faith they chose.

2. Based on the image, how did Penn treat American Indians?

   _____

   _____

   _____

   _____

3. If you were a settler coming to America, do you think you would choose to live around Philadelphia? Why or why not?

   _____

   _____

   _____

   _____

Civics

Name: _____ **Date:** _____

Directions: Look at the image, and answer the question.

Colonists solved community problems at town hall meetings. They passed laws for citizens to follow. They set budgets and taxes. The meetings usually took place once a year.

1. How does your classroom or family use the model of a town hall meeting? Or, if it doesn't, why might that be a good idea?

_____

_____

_____

_____

_____

_____

_____

Name: _____ **Date:** _____

Directions: Read the text, and answer the questions.

In the 1600s, people risked their lives crossing the Atlantic Ocean. They came from different countries. They were brave and hopeful. Some of them came to practice their faith in their own way. Puritans left Britain to gain this freedom. Other settlers wanted to own land. Adventurers searched for silver and gold. Explorers and traders came. They traded with American Indians.

The British king let groups of settlers start colonies along the Atlantic coast. It took 125 years to settle 13 colonies. In 1607, Virginia became the first colony. In 1732, Georgia was the last colony.

arriving in Jamestown, Virginia, 1607

1. Why did Puritans come to America?
   a. They needed to get more food to eat.
   b. They came to gain religious freedom.
   c. They hoped to find silver and gold.
   d. They wanted to become fur traders.

2. Where were the 13 colonies located?
   a. around the Gulf of Mexico
   b. along the Pacific Ocean
   c. near the Great Lakes
   d. along the Atlantic coast

3. Based on the text, how were the people who came to America brave? Circle all that apply.
   a. They risked their lives crossing the ocean.
   b. They were ready to face the unknown.
   c. They were leaving their families behind.
   d. They had to start all over again.

Name: _____ Date: _____

Directions: Review the chart, and answer the questions.

Geography

Settlement of the 13 Colonies			
Colony	**Year**	**Founders**	**First Settlements**
Virginia	1607	London Company	British
Massachusetts	1620	Puritans (Pilgrims)	British
New Hampshire	1622	John Mason, Ferdinando Gorges, and John Wheelwright	British
Maryland	1632	Cecil Calvert	British
Connecticut	1633	Thomas Hooker	Dutch in 1614, then British
Rhode Island	1647	Roger Williams	British
Delaware	1638	Peter Minuit and New Sweden Company	Dutch in 1631, Swedish in 1638, then British
North Carolina	1653	Virginians	British
South Carolina	1663	Royal Charter from Charles II	British
New Jersey	1664	Lord Berkeley and Sir George Carteret	Dutch, Swedes, and Finns, then British
New York	1664	Duke of York	Dutch, then British
Pennsylvania	1681	William Penn	Swedes in 1638, Dutch in 1655, then British
Georgia	1732	James Oglethorpe	British

1. From 1607 to 1732, who made the most settlements?

   a. the Puritans

   b. the Dutch

   c. the British

   d. the Swedes

2. How did New York get its name? Circle the best answer.

   a. It was named after a Dutch king.

   b. Colonists named it after a British city.

   c. Colonists described all their land as "new."

   d. It was named after the Duke of York.

3. How much time passed between the founding of the first British colony and the last?

   a. 25 years

   b. 150 years

   c. 55 years

   d. 125 years

51397—180 Days of Social Studies

© *Shell Education*

Name: _____ Date:_____

Directions: Review the chart, and answer the questions.

The 13 Colonies as Geographic Regions			
Colonies	**Geography**	**Natural Resources**	**Climate**
New England Colonies Connecticut Rhode Island Massachusetts New Hampshire	mountains thick with trees, rivers, and rocky soil that was hard to farm	fish, whales, forests (logging, shipbuilding), furs	coldest of the three regions, with harsher winters and warm summers
Middle Colonies Delaware Pennsylvania New Jersey New York	plains along the coastline, rolling hills in the middle, and mountains farther inland	good farmland for wheat, timber, furs, coal, iron ore	temperate, with warm summers and cold winters
Southern Colonies Maryland Virginia North Carolina South Carolina Georgia	fertile soil, hilly coastal plains, forests, long rivers, flat land, and swamp areas	fish, forests (timber), good fertile flat land suitable for growing cotton, tobacco, rice, indigo	warm to hot climate, with a long growing season

1. Where is the best place for farming?

   a. Georgia

   b. Rhode Island

   c. New York

   d. New Hampshire

2. In what colony did people mine for coal and iron ore?

   a. Connecticut

   b. Pennsylvania

   c. South Carolina

   d. Maryland

3. Imagine that you are going to settle in America. Which colony would you choose? Why?

   _____

   _____

   _____

   _____

Geography

Name: _____ **Date:** _____

Directions: Review the chart, and answer the questions.

Geography

What Pilgrims Packed	
Food and Drink	biscuits, beer, salt, dried beef, salt pork, oats, peas, wheat, butter, sweet oil, mustard seed, cod fish, cheese, vinegar, rice, bacon
Household Goods	iron pot, kettle, frying pan, gridiron, two skillets, platters, dishes, wooden spoons, napkins, towels, soap, hand mill
Tools	hoes, axe, steel handsaw, hammers, shovels, chisels, hatchets, grinding stone, nails, locks for doors

1. What food group is missing from the list?

   a. meat

   b. dairy

   c. vegetables

   d. fruit

2. Review the list of tools. What types of work do you think the Pilgrims expected to do?

_____

_____

_____

3. Some household goods and tools used in the 1600s are also used today. What household goods and tools do your family members use?

Household Goods	Tools

Name: _____ **Date:** _____

Directions: Read the chart. Sketch and label the map.

The Three Colonial Regions		
New England Colonies	**Middle Colonies**	**Southern Colonies**
Connecticut Rhode Island Massachusetts New Hampshire	Delaware Pennsylvania New Jersey New York	Maryland Virginia North Carolina South Carolina Georgia

1. Use the outline below. Label each of the 13 colonies. Label the Atlantic Ocean.

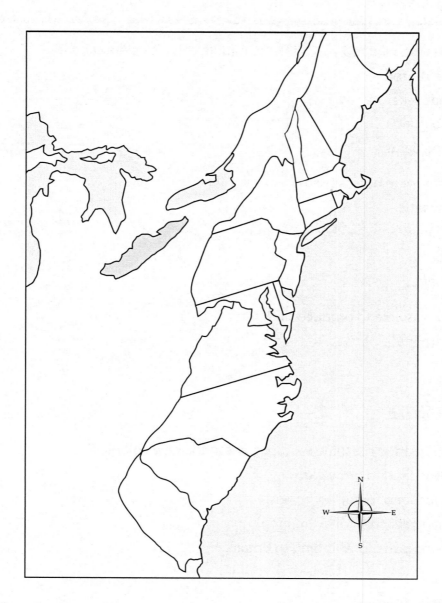

Geography

Economics

Name: _____ Date: _____

Directions: Read the text, and answer the questions.

> There were three areas in the 13 colonies. Each was different because of its geography. The New England colonies had many trees, so the settlers built a lot of sawmills. Shipbuilders used the lumber. These colonies had a long coastline. They had many places to build ports.
>
> The middle colonies also had ports along their coast. They grew lots of wheat and rye. These crops enabled colonists to make bread. They mined iron. They used hemp to make textiles. Paper was made in Philadelphia. Horses were bred in New Jersey.
>
> In the southern colonies, plantations grew rice, tobacco, and indigo. Silk was produced in Georgia. Bricks, barrels, and pottery were made. Traders shipped goods to Britain at ocean ports.

1. Based on the text, what do you think the middle colonies were called?
   a. the trade center
   b. the breadbasket
   c. the rice basket
   d. the fishing center

2. In what colony were horses bred?
   a. Massachusetts
   b. Pennsylvania
   c. Georgia
   d. New Jersey

3. What colony was able to produce silk?
   a. South Carolina
   b. Virginia
   c. Georgia
   d. North Carolina

4. Why was the Atlantic coastline so important to the new colonies?
   a. It was good land to grow crops.
   b. It was good land for racing horses.
   c. It had many beaches for swimming.
   d. It had many ports for shipping to Britain.

70

© *Shell Education*

Name: _____ **Date:** _____

Directions: Read the text, and answer the questions.

William Rittenhouse settled near Philadelphia, Pennsylvania, in 1690. He built a paper mill and began to make paper. It didn't cost much to make paper in the colonies. Before then, all paper had been imported from Britain.

The paper was made from old rags and cotton. Power from a waterwheel beat the rags into a pulp. The pulp was spread on screens. The screens were hung to dry. This paper mill was the only one in the colonies for 20 years.

1. Before 1690, where did colonists get their paper?

   a. New York   **c.** Philadelphia

   b. Britain   **d.** Canada

2. What was used to make paper?

   a. sawdust

   b. tree pulp

   c. rags and cotton

   d. straw and hay

3. Based on the text, how would a paper mill help the colonies?

   a. Printers could share their texts and ideas more easily.

   b. Paper would cost less than bringing it from Britain.

   c. The mill provided an early way to recycle.

   d. The mill gave work to people at home in America.

4. Name three ways that paper would have been used in the colonies.

   _____

   _____

   _____

Economics

Name:_____ Date:_____

Directions: Read the chart, and view the image. Answer the questions.

Ships Built in the New England and Middle Colonies, 1674–1714			
Massachusetts	1,246	Maryland	185
Pennsylvania	226	New Hampshire	769

1. Based on the chart, where did the most shipbuilders live between 1674 and 1714?

   a. New Hampshire   **c.** Maryland

   b. Massachusetts   **d.** Pennsylvania

2. Based on the image, describe the material and tools that are needed to build a ship.

   _____

   _____

   _____

3. Why would these shipbuilders build a ship at this location?

   _____

   _____

   _____

Name: _____ **Date:** _____

Directions: Study the picture, and answer the questions.

Women in colonial times lived different lives than they do today. They had jobs to do throughout the year. These jobs kept them working from dawn to dusk. Girls worked alongside their mothers at home.

Women also worked in their gardens. They would grow vegetables in the summer. The food would be harvested in the fall.

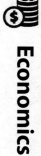

Economics

1. What were girls expected to do?

 a. play outside all day

 b. go to school to learn to read

 c. find nuts and wild berries

 d. help their mothers with work

2. Imagine that you live in colonial times. Describe a job you would like to do in and around the home.

 _____

 _____

 _____

3. Compare the life of a woman in a colonial home with the life of a woman today.

 _____

 _____

 _____

 _____

Economics

Name:_____ Date:_____

Directions: Review the map, and answer the question.

Natural Resources in the 13 Colonies

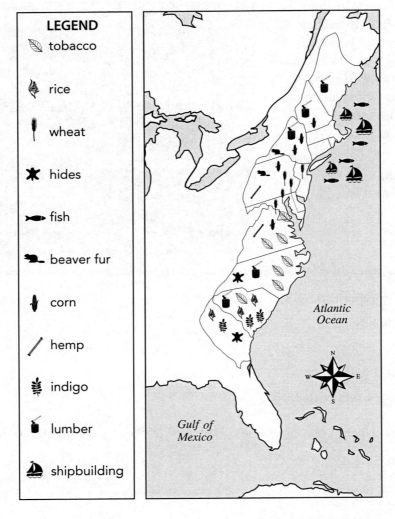

1. Explain how the industries are based on the geography in the colonies?

_____

_____

_____

_____

_____

Name: _____ **Date:** _____

Directions: Read the text, and answer the questions.

France and Britain were at war in Europe. This war spread to North America. Both countries had colonies there. They also had armies. Each country wanted to control the Ohio Valley. This area looked good for trade and settlement. The French and Indian War began in 1754.

George Washington became famous while fighting in this war. He was a major in the Virginia militia. He led the attack that started the war. He helped the British army fight the French. American Indians fought on both the French and British sides.

Then, the Treaty of Paris ended the war in 1763. France lost most of its land in North America to Britain. Britain gained all land east of the Mississippi. Spain got all land west of the Mississippi.

Washington during the French and Indian War

1. Which army did Washington support during the French and Indian War?
   a. American
   b. French
   c. British
   d. Spanish

2. What treaty ended the French and Indian War?
   a. the French–Indian Treaty
   b. the Treaty of Paris
   c. the American Treaty
   d. the Treaty of Washington

3. What did Britain get from the peace treaty? Circle all that apply.
   a. land that had belonged to France
   b. land west of the Mississippi
   c. land east of the Mississippi
   d. islands in the Caribbean

Name: _____ Date: _____

History

Directions: Read the text, and answer the questions.

The French and Indian War was fought on the North American continent. The British won that war. They also won the Seven Years War. This was the war fought in Europe and around the world.

The wars cost Britain a lot of money. Britain couldn't pay to ship its soldiers home. It also couldn't pay to house them in America. So the king passed the Quartering Act. Colonists had to provide the soldiers with food and shelter.

Soldiers would stay in all kinds of buildings, such as barracks, public houses, inns, and barns. Looking after the British troops made the colonists unhappy. Having an army of British soldiers in America upset them.

British soldiers quartered in a colonial home

1. Who won the Seven Years War?
   a. the French
   b. the American Indians
   c. the British
   d. the Americans

2. What did the Quartering Act make the colonists do?
   a. ship the British soldiers home
   b. provide soldiers with food and housing
   c. pay the soldiers a wage while in America
   d. give Britain money for the cost of the wars

3. What was one effect of the Quartering Act on the colonists?
   a. It left British troops in the colonies after the war.
   b. It helped colonists and soldiers get along better.
   c. It made colonists grateful for the protection.
   d. It worried colonists that a new war would start.

51397—180 Days of Social Studies

© *Shell Education*

Name: _____ **Date:** _____

Directions: Read the diagram, and answer the questions.

1st Continental Congress, 1774
- outlined colonial rights
- listed how Britain violated their rights
- told Britain they were unhappy with taxes
- agreed not to buy British goods
- discussed forming a national government

- 12 of 13 colonies
- Georgia did not send delegate.
- John Adams and Thomas Jefferson led the drive for a national government.

2nd Continental Congress, 1775
- agreed to act as national government
- made plans to separate from Britain
- appointed George Washington as commander of the Continental Army
- agreed that each colony would create its own militia (volunteer soldiers)
- led to American Revolution

1. Who wanted a national government? Circle all that apply.

   a. George Washington

   b. John Adams

   c. James Madison

   d. Thomas Jefferson

2. Why did the colonists meet in 1774?

   _____

   _____

   _____

3. What did the colonial leaders do in 1775?

   _____

   _____

   _____

Name: _____ Date: _____

History

Directions: Read the text, and answer the questions.

George Washington grew up on a tobacco plantation. He was 21 when he fought in the French and Indian War. He then married Martha Custis. They lived at Mount Vernon.

Washington was a leader all his life. He was elected to the Virginia legislature. He believed that the colonies should split from Britain. During the American Revolution, he served as a general for the Continental Army. He developed a spy network to gather news about the British. This effort helped win the war.

Washington was elected as the first president of the United States. He served for two terms.

Washington at Mount Vernon

1. Based on the text, what did George Washington do? Circle all that apply.
   a. He fought in the Civil War.
   b. He fought in the French and Indian War.
   c. He served as the first U.S. president.
   d. He lived at Mount Vernon with his wife.

2. What was one way Washington helped during the American Revolution?
   a. He developed a spy network.
   b. He served as a major in the army.
   c. He stayed at Mount Vernon.
   d. He became the American president.

3. Washington is a good role model for leadership. How can you be a leader in your family or school community?

   _____

   _____

   _____

   _____

Name: _____ **Date:** _____

Directions: Read the text, and answer the question.

Paul Revere was a Boston silversmith. He also played a secret role as a mechanic. He helped to create a spy network to keep track of British army plans.

Mechanics kept watch on the British army and people known to be loyal to it. They patrolled the streets. They watched for troop movements. To pass on messages, they used a series of lanterns. They were the "Liberty Boys."

Paul Revere on his midnight ride

1. Paul Revere is best known for his midnight ride to Lexington. He warned people that the British were coming. Today, neighborhood groups watch out for people in different ways. What group in your neighborhood does this? What do they do, and how?

_____

_____

_____

_____

_____

_____

_____

_____

_____

Name: _____ **Date:** _____

Civics

Directions: Read the text, and answer the questions.

In 1776, the Americans wrote the Declaration of Independence. It listed the rights and freedoms of its citizens. Long before that, in 1689, the British had the Bill of Rights. It supported basic rights that individuals should have. It gave people more liberty. They had greater freedom to do and say what they wanted to.

The document gave citizens the right to hold free elections. Men elected Parliament. Taxes were voted on by Parliament. The document also helped to protect people. It put a stop to huge fines. It stopped cruel and unusual punishment by the courts. It declared that there could be no full-time army in times of peace.

King William and Queen Mary give the British Bill of Rights royal approval.

1. How were the members of Parliament selected?

   a. The king chose the members.

   b. Women voted for the members.

   c. Men voted for Parliament.

   d. People volunteered for Parliament.

2. How were taxes determined?

   a. They were voted on in Parliament.

   b. They were set by the king.

   c. They were voted on by rich citizens.

   d. They were set by a special committee.

3. What does the word *liberty* mean?

   a. life

   b. an idea

   c. a goddess

   d. freedom

51397—180 Days of Social Studies

Name: _____ **Date:** _____

Directions: Read the text, and answer the questions.

The Sons of Liberty was a secret group that formed before the American Revolution. Its goal was to protect colonists' rights. Its motto became "No taxation without representation."

The Sons of Liberty met to protest the payment of British Stamp Act taxes. They gathered under an elm tree in Boston. The tree became known as the "Liberty Tree." The group continued to meet under the tree. The British cut it down. The group set up a Liberty pole. They flew their flag from the pole. The flag's vertical lines represented nine colonies that united against the British tax rules.

colonists meeting at the Liberty Tree

1. Why did the Sons of Liberty form?

   a. to plant an elm tree in Boston

   b. to protect the rights of colonists

   c. to pay taxes to Britain

   d. to create a special flag

2. What replaced the Liberty Tree?

   a. the Liberty stamp

   b. the Liberty flag

   c. the Liberty pole

   d. the Liberty oak

3. Why did the British cut down the elm?

   a. They didn't want it to provide shade.

   b. The tree was diseased.

   c. The tree was the site of protests.

   d. Colonists had parties beneath it.

Civics

Name: _____ **Date:** _____

Directions: Read the text, look at the graphic, and answer the questions.

In December 1775, Benjamin Franklin wrote this in the *Pennsylvania Gazette*:

No eye-lids so she is always on the watch, always vigilant.

Doesn't begin an attack, but once in battle, she doesn't surrender.

Her defenses are hidden (in her mouth) so she appears weak.

And though the bite is small, it's deadly.

She doesn't attack until after she gives warning.

THE CULPEPER MINUTE MEN

LIBERTY OR DEATH

DONT TREAD ON ME

1. Who does this flag represent?

   a. the Continental Army   **c.** all minute men in the colonies

   b. all patriots in the colonies   **d.** the Culpeper Minute Men

2. The men want liberty. How determined are they to get it? Explain.

_____

_____

_____

3. Why was the rattlesnake a good symbol? Be sure to consider Franklin's words.

_____

_____

_____

82

Name: _____ **Date:** _____

Directions: Read the text, and answer the questions.

Civics

Women helped fight for freedom. In 1765, Boston women formed the Daughters of Liberty. Women could not vote at that time. However, they could do other things to make a difference in politics.

The women supported the goals of the Sons of Liberty. The men were protesting the high taxes in the colonies. The women began their own protests. They boycotted British goods. They refused to drink British tea. Instead, they drank "liberty tea." This tea was brewed with berries and herbs. The women wove cloth and spun their own yarn, too. That meant they needed less from Britain.

1. The Daughters of Liberty created a tea. What was its name?
   a. berry tea
   b. herbal tea
   c. liberty tea
   d. British tea

2. How did the Daughters of Liberty support the cause of the Sons of Liberty?
   a. They stayed home and let the men protest.
   b. They stayed home and drank tea.
   c. They read about events in the news.
   d. They avoided buying British goods.

3. How can you support a good cause in your community or in your country?

   _____

   _____

   _____

   _____

Name:_____ Date:_____

Civics

Directions: Look at text and images. Answer the question.

American colonists were British citizens. However, no one represented them in British Parliament. Some colonists wanted to break away from Britain. They were called *patriots*. These colonists felt that the government was ignoring their rights. British laws made the colonies pay high taxes. They also told the colonists to house and feed British soldiers. Colonists didn't like being told what to do.

Other colonists did not want to break away from Britain. They were called *loyalists*. Some colonists did business with Britain. They wanted to continue to do so. Loyalists believed that British rule was best.

British flag, 1776   U.S. flag, 1776

1. What did the patriots and loyalists have in common? How did they differ? Refer to the text above to complete the diagram.

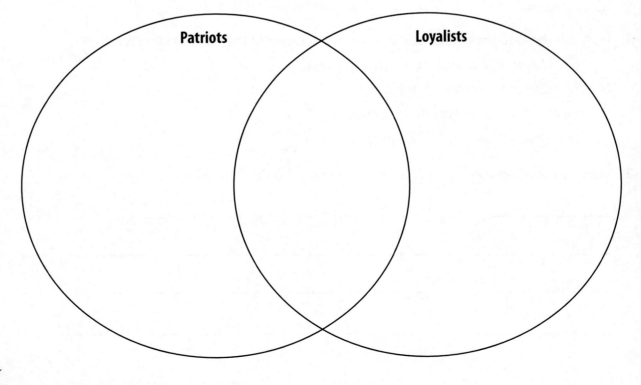

Patriots   Loyalists

Name: _____ **Date:** _____

Directions: Read the text, and study the map. Answer the questions.

Major Port Cities in the 13 Colonies

Port cities were important in the colonies. They were places of trade and commerce. They were hubs for shipping goods to Europe. The wealth of each colony depended on them.

Ports provided work. Merchants, wholesalers, agents, and sailors took part in shipping. Shopkeepers and tradespeople were needed, too.

Each of the three colonial regions had at least one major port. Boston was the main port of the New England colonies. New York City, Philadelphia, and Baltimore were key ports in the middle colonies. Charleston was the main port for the southern colonies.

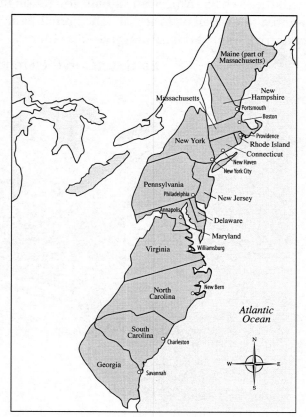

1. Circle these ports on the map: Boston, Philadelphia, New York City, and Charleston.

2. In what colony was Boston located?
   a. New Hampshire
   b. Massachusetts
   c. Rhode Island
   d. Connecticut

3. Why were ports so important in the 13 colonies? Circle the best answer.
   a. Everyone owned a boat in these cities.
   b. They were centers for shipping across the Atlantic.
   c. Shipping was the only business in the colonies.
   d. They were the best places to build ships.

Geography

Name: _____ **Date:** _____

Directions: Read the text, and study the map. Answer the questions.

It was the time of the French and Indian War in America. The British were at war with the French. American Indians fought on both sides. Both Britain and France wanted to own all of America. The French built a lot of forts in the Ohio Country. Both countries wanted the natural resources there.

Battle Sites in the French and Indian War

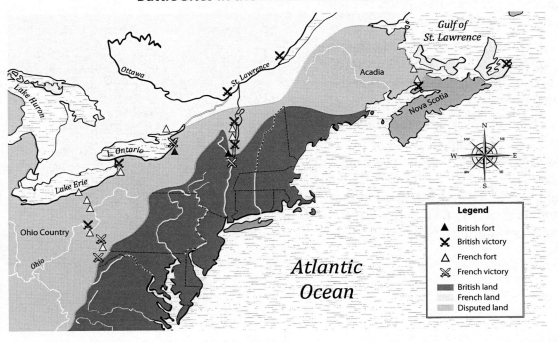

1. Review the map. Who won the most battles in the war?

   a. the French   **c.** the American Indians

   b. the British   **d.** the Americans

2. Based on this map, who held the land north of the Great Lakes?

   a. the British   **c.** the French

   b. the Acadians   **d.** the American Indians

3. The map shows three land areas. In which land area were most battles fought? Why is that so?

   _____

   _____

   _____

Name: _____ **Date:** _____

Directions: Study the map, and answer the questions.

Triangular Trade

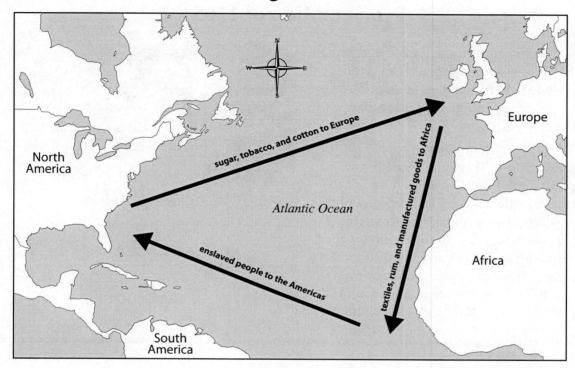

1. What was shipped from America to Europe?

   a. enslaved people

   b. rum

   c. tobacco

   d. textiles

2. What was shipped from Africa to America?

   a. sugar

   b. cotton

   c. sugar

   d. enslaved people

3. Why was this trade pattern called "triangular trade"? What did it depend on?

   _____

   _____

   _____

Name:_____ Date:_____

Geography

Directions: Read the text, and study the map. Answer the questions.

Proclamation of 1763

Britain had won the French and Indian War. It now owned the land that France had long held in North America. Colonists and American Indian supporters had helped Britain win.

In 1763, Britain made a royal proclamation. This announcement set a north–south line. Colonists were not to cross or settle past it. The land west of the Appalachians was meant for American Indians. Britain hoped to remain on good terms with its American Indian supporters. It knew American Indians did not want colonists taking over their land. Colonists moving west of the line would be sent back.

1. How did the Proclamation of 1763 affect colonists?

   a. It gave land to all Britain's supporters.

   b. It forced American Indians to move east of the line.

   c. Colonists could not move west of the line.

   d. Colonists had to share new land with American Indians.

2. What defined the Proclamation line?

   a. the length of the Mississippi River

   b. the size of the 13 colonies

   c. the Appalachian Mountains

   d. the importance of American Indian support

3. Do you think the British should have set aside this land for its American Indian supporters? Why or why not?

   _____

   _____

© Shell Education

Name: _____ **Date:** _____

Directions: Study the two images, and complete the Venn diagram.

Southern plantation owners and their families lived very differently from the slave families that served them.

Plantation Owner Home and Family   **Slave Home and Family**

Economics

Name: _____ Date: _____

Directions: Read the text, and answer the questions.

The 13 colonies had natural resources that Britain needed. The colonies shipped lots of furs, lumber, iron ore, and fish to Britain. They also grew tobacco, indigo, rice, and wheat. They shipped these resources across the ocean, too. Britain sent back products made from the resources. The colonists had to pay for the products. The British set the prices. Colonists were not allowed to trade with each other. They could not trade with other countries, either.

Britain controlled trade with its colonies. The colonists did not like this control. They wanted to make their own trade decisions.

1. What natural resources did the colonies send to Britain? Circle all that apply.

   a. furs and lumber

   b. paper and cardboard

   c. tea and oranges

   d. tobacco and iron ore

2. What did Britain send to the colonies?

   a. fur hats and clothes

   b. iron ore and fish

   c. rice and wheat

   d. lumber and furs

3. Who controlled trade in the colonies?

   a. the British government

   b. the colonial governments

   c. the French government

   d. the American government

4. Based on the text, what was the main problem with buying products from Britain?

   a. It was hard to get a refund.

   b. The products were of poor quality.

   c. Delivery took a long time.

   d. The British set the prices.

Name:_____ **Date:**_____

Directions: Read the text and chart, and answer the questions.

British Tax Acts	
Dates and Names	**What the Acts Did**
1651: Navigation Acts	It set trade rules for the colonies.
1764: Sugar Act	Sugar and molasses from countries other than Britain are taxed.
1765: Quartering Act	Colonists must house and feed British troops.
1765: Stamp Act	Legal documents, paper, newspapers, and pamphlets are taxed.
1773: Tea Act	Colonists have to buy tea from one British company only and pay tax.
1774: Intolerable Acts	Five laws make British power over the colonies stronger.

  Each colony had its own government. It dealt with day-to-day laws. Britain was 4,000 miles away. The king could send messages to the colonies only by ship. It took weeks for a message to cross the ocean. The colonies had to act on their own.

  Britain wanted to control what went on in the colonies. The British government passed many acts to collect taxes from the colonists.

1. What act made colonists pay taxes on paper?

 a. Quartering Act

 b. Tea Act

 c. Stamp Act

 d. Sugar Act

2. What act made the colonists house and feed British troops?

 a. Quartering Act

 b. Tea Act

 c. Stamp Act

 d. Sugar Act

3. Why did the British pass so many acts?

_____

_____

_____

Name: _____ Date: _____

Economics

Directions: Review the map, and answer the questions.

The Enslaved Population in 1770

400 km
200 mi

New Hampshire 654
Massachusetts 4,754
New York 19,062
Rhode Island 3,761
Connecticut 5,698
Pennsylvania 5,561
New Jersey 8,220
Delaware 1,836
Virginia 187,600
Maryland 63,818
69,600 North Carolina
75,178 South Carolina
Georgia 15,000

1. In 1770, which colony had the fewest enslaved people?
   a. Delaware
   b. Virginia
   c. New Hampshire
   d. North Carolina

2. In 1770, which colony had almost 20,000 enslaved people?
   a. Georgia
   b. Connecticut
   c. Pennsylvania
   d. New York

3. In 1770, which small colony had a large enslaved population?
   a. Delaware
   b. Maryland
   c. New Jersey
   d. Rhode Island

4. Look at Virginia and Pennsylvania on the map. How do the numbers of enslaved people compare? Why?

_____

_____

_____

_____

_____

Name: _____ **Date:** _____

Directions: Read the text, and answer the questions.

> The British passed five harsh acts. Colonists called them the "Intolerable Acts." They felt badly treated.
>
> - **Boston Port Act:** The British closed the Boston port. Colonists had to pay taxes on the tea that tax protesters had thrown into the harbor.
> - **Massachusetts Government Act:** The British governor gained greater power. He did not have to hold elections. Colonists could hold a town hall meeting only once a year.
> - **Administration of Justice Act:** The governor could move criminal trials out of the colonies. That was a way to protect British officials accused of serious crimes. It would be hard for witnesses to attend.
> - **Quartering Act:** Colonists might have to give room and board to British soldiers in their barns, hotels, and homes.
> - **Quebec Act:** The British now controlled Quebec. The act recognized the French-speaking province as Roman Catholic. It also made the Ohio Valley part of it. Colonists had hoped to settle there.

1. How were colonists punished by the Boston Port Act?
   a. Town hall meetings could take place only yearly.
   b. Colonists had to pay taxes on tea thrown off ships.
   c. Witnesses to serious crimes could not sail to trials in Britain.
   d. Colonists had to house troops without payment.

2. Why did colonists find the Massachusetts Government Act "intolerable"?
   a. Colonists had to become Roman Catholic.
   b. Everyone had to pay tax on tea in Boston.
   c. The British governor did not have to hold elections.
   d. The governor could shift trials to Britain.

3. Think of a rule at home or school you disagree with. What is it? How do you think it should be changed?

_____

_____

_____

_____

Economics

Name: _____ **Date:** _____

Directions: Look at the image, and read the text. Answer the question.

The Boston Tea Party

    Britain had set high taxes on tea. At this time, the colonists drank a lot of it. All their tea came from Britain. The taxes angered them.

    Samuel Adams organized what became known as the "Boston Tea Party." The Sons of Liberty and other patriots took part. More than 100 men boarded three tea ships in Boston Harbor. They tossed more than 300 crates of tea into the water.

1. Look at the ship scene. What are the men doing? How is this "party" a protest?

_____

_____

_____

_____

_____

_____

51397—180 Days of Social Studies

Name: _____ Date: _____

Directions: Read the text, and answer the questions.

Colonists were at war with Britain in the American Revolution. A group was formed to spy on the British. Benjamin Tallmadge was its leader. Friends helped him. A shop owner in New York gathered information. A trader smuggled it out. A whaleboat captain delivered it to George Washington. This group was the Culper Spy Ring.

Men and women in disguise collected information. Women hung laundry of different colors to give news about message pickup. Spies wrote notes in invisible ink. John Jay made dictionary codes to send secret messages. Charles Dumas made a cipher with numbers and letters. This code was added to documents. Spies used it to understand messages.

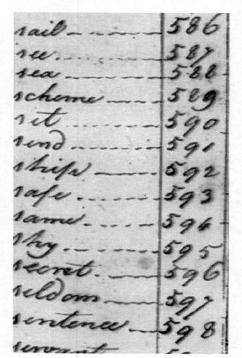

This key code was sent to George Washington.

History

1. How did women help spy on the British? Circle all that apply.
   a. They sailed on whale ships.
   b. They hung laundry outside.
   c. They wrote documents.
   d. They disguised themselves.

2. What are ciphers?
   a. codes used for hanging laundry
   b. codes based on letters only
   c. codes with letters and numbers
   d. codes needing dictionary use

3. Who was the leader of the group that spied against the British?
   a. Charles Dumas
   b. John Jay
   c. George Washington
   d. Benjamin Tallmadge

Name:_____ Date:_____

History

Directions: Read the text , and answer the questions.

Deborah Sampson became a hero of the American Revolution. Disguised as a man, she joined the Continental Army. She became a scout. Her job was to watch the buildup of British soldiers and materials in Manhattan. George Washington was planning an attack. She led a raid and captured 15 loyalists.

Sampson stayed in the army until her gender was discovered. She kept her secret when she got wounded. But, when she got ill, they found out she was a woman. She received an honorable discharge.

Sampson giving Washington a letter

1. How was Deborah Sampson able to join the military?

   a. She volunteered in her community.

   b. She disguised herself as a man.

   c. Her father signed her up for service.

   d. The army allowed women to join.

2. Based on the text, how did Sampson show her bravery in the revolution?

   a. She served as a scout close to the British army.

   b. She fought in the trenches outside Yorktown.

   c. She told George Washington to hire women soldiers.

   d. She led a raid and captured 15 loyalists.

3. Sampson is a hero to Americans. Why?

   _____

   _____

   _____

   _____

96

© *Shell Education*

Name: _____ **Date:** _____

Directions: Study the diagram, and answer the questions.

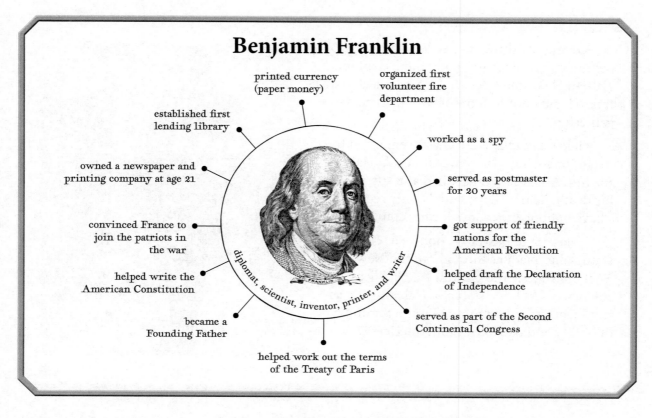

Benjamin Franklin

printed currency (paper money)

organized first volunteer fire department

established first lending library

worked as a spy

owned a newspaper and printing company at age 21

served as postmaster for 20 years

convinced France to join the patriots in the war

got support of friendly nations for the American Revolution

helped write the American Constitution

helped draft the Declaration of Independence

became a Founding Father

served as part of the Second Continental Congress

helped work out the terms of the Treaty of Paris

diplomat, scientist, inventor, printer, and writer

1. Benjamin Franklin did many things in his life. What did he NOT do?

   a. help draft the Declaration of Independence

   b. own a newspaper and print shop

   c. become a key Founding Father of the United States

   d. serve as president of the United States

2. To *negotiate* means to work something out by talking. How did Franklin show he had good negotiating skills?

   _____

   _____

   _____

3. What did Franklin's writing skills help him do?

   _____

   _____

History

Name: _____ Date: _____

Directions: Read the text, and answer the questions.

George Washington needed a spy to go behind enemy lines in Manhattan. Captain Nathan Hale volunteered. He was brave to do this. He was not well trained in intelligence gathering.

Hale was captured. He was sentenced to death for spying. There was no trial. Hale was the first American to be killed as a spy. Before his death, he may have said, "I only regret that I have but one life to lose for my country."

Hale's act of bravery is honored with statues and plaques throughout the New England states. The Central Intelligence Agency (CIA) has a statue of Hale outside its headquarters. The monument is a reminder of liberty and patriotism for Americans.

1. What was one reason Hale was not a successful spy?
   a. He had little help with the mission.
   b. He did not have enough training.
   c. He needed more information.
   d. He went to the wrong location.

2. Why does the CIA honor Hale?

   _____

   _____

   _____

3. How do you show that you are brave?

   _____

   _____

   _____

Name: _____ **Date:** _____

Directions: Look at the image, and answer the question.

"GOOD-BYE, WHIGGIES."

*A troop of British redcoat soldiers wave to a loyalist family
during the American Revolution.*

1. What do you think the loyalist family would do if colonial soldiers were marching in their area? Give reasons for your answer.

_____

_____

_____

_____

_____

_____

_____

_____

_____

_____

Name: _____ **Date:** _____

Civics

Directions: Read the text, and answer the questions.

People around Boston did not like British laws. A group of men wrote their complaints. These complaints were called the "Suffolk Resolves." Townspeople protested the acts that Britain had passed. They refused to pay taxes. They avoided trading with Britain. Volunteers trained with guns every week. These actions were against British law.

Paul Revere delivered the written complaints to the First Continental Congress in Philadelphia. Many people were now showing their anger with Britain.

Paul Revere

1. Why did people around Boston write the Suffolk Resolves?
   a. to share their willingness to obey British laws in the colonies
   b. to list rules to follow to show their loyalty to the king
   c. to show their happiness with the government of Britain
   d. to express what they felt about recent British acts

2. Who delivered the Suffolk Resolves to Philadelphia?
   a. George Washington
   b. Paul Revere
   c. Samuel Adams
   d. Benjamin Franklin

3. What did people do to show how they felt toward Britain? Circle all that apply.
   a. They broke the laws.
   b. They started training to fight.
   c. They did not pay taxes.
   d. They traded with Britain.

Name: _____ **Date:** _____

Directions: Read the text, and answer the questions.

Thomas Paine wanted a better life. Benjamin Franklin persuaded him to move from Britain to Philadelphia to find it. Paine was interested in the revolution just starting in America. George Washington liked his thinking.

Paine wrote a pamphlet, *Common Sense*. He wanted to convince people to break from British rule. His writing was clear and easy to read. Some people could not read, however. They heard *Common Sense* read aloud. The pamphlet got colonists talking about their dislike of Britain. It helped rally them to support the revolution.

COMMON SENSE;
ADDRESSED TO THE
INHABITANTS
OF
AMERICA,
On the following interesting
SUBJECTS.

I. Of the Origin and Defign of Government in general,
with concife Remarks on the Englifh Conftitution.

II. Of Monarchy and Hereditary Succeffion.

III. Thoughts on the prefent State of American Affairs.

IV. Of the prefent Ability of America, with fome mif-
cellaneous Reflections.

Man knows no Mafter fave creaing HEAVEN,
Or thofe whom choice and common good ordain.
THOMSON.

1. Based on the text, why did Thomas Paine write his pamphlet?
   a. to have a better life in America
   b. to gain support for the revolution
   c. to sell as many copies as possible
   d. to make George Washington happy

2. Based on the text, how do you know the pamphlet was a success?
   a. It was easy to read.
   b. George Washington liked it.
   c. Paine was a famous author.
   d. People talked about it.

3. Look at the image. To whom is *Common Sense* addressed?
   a. to people who live in Britain
   b. to people who live in Philadelphia
   c. to inhabitants of America
   d. to colonial college students

Civics

Name: _____ **Date:** _____

Directions: Look at the image, and answer the questions.

The Declaration of Independence

IN CONGRESS. JULY 4, 1776.

The unanimous Declaration of the thirteen united States of America,

1. The man with the largest handwriting was first to sign it. Who was he?

   a. John Dickinson   **c.** Benjamin Franklin

   b. John Hancock   **d.** John Adams

2. How well did Congress members agree on the Declaration? Look at the top of the document.

   a. They all agreed.   **c.** They agreed to disagree.

   b. They did not agree.   **d.** They were forced to agree.

3. Why do you think that Congress had the document printed in colonial newspapers and read aloud?

   _____

   _____

   _____

Name: _____ **Date:** _____

Directions: Read the text, and answer the questions.

The Treaty of Paris ended the American Revolution. People from both sides signed it on September 3, 1783 in Paris, France. John Adams, John Jay, and Benjamin Franklin signed it for the United States. David Hartley signed it for Britain.

The treaty signing was an important world event. The Americans sat for a painting of it. The British refused to sit. The painting was never finished.

This unfinished painting shows how divided the United States and Britain were.

1. Where was the treaty signed?

   a. United States

   b. Britain

   c. France

   d. the colonies

2. Why do you think no one from Britain would sit for the painting?

   _____

   _____

   _____

3. How does your family remember important events?

   _____

   _____

   _____

Civics

Name:_____ **Date:**_____

Directions: Read the infographic, and answer the question.

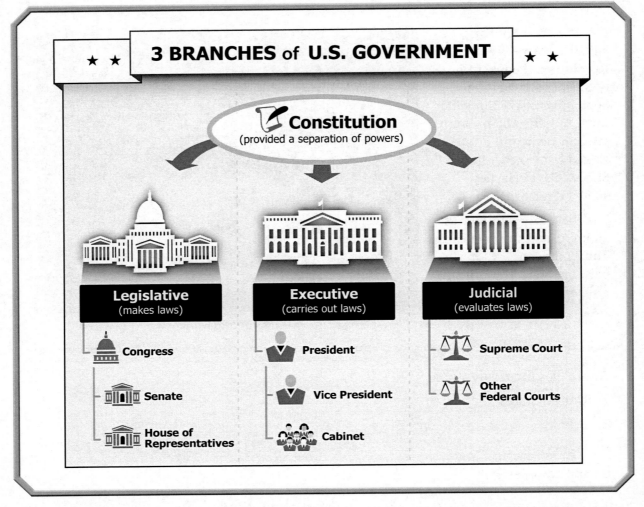

3 BRANCHES of U.S. GOVERNMENT

Constitution
(provided a separation of powers)

Legislative
(makes laws)

Executive
(carries out laws)

Judicial
(evaluates laws)

Congress

President

Supreme Court

Senate

Vice President

Other
Federal Courts

House of
Representatives

Cabinet

1. The American Revolution resulted in a new government. The U.S. Constitution was written in 1787. It set up a national government with three branches. Why did the leaders create a new type of government?

_____

_____

_____

_____

_____

_____

Name: _____ **Date:** _____

Directions: Read the text, and study the map. Answer the questions.

The Battles of Lexington and Concord started the American Revolution. The British wanted to capture Samuel Adams and John Hancock. Americans learned of their plans. Paul Revere rode out to Lexington late at night to warn the two men. Adams and Hancock escaped. The British army marched into Lexington. Neither side expected a battle, but a shot went off—"the shot heard around the world." The British wanted to destroy American guns and ammunition. They marched toward Concord. So did militiamen. The guns and ammunition were hidden. The British retreated to Boston.

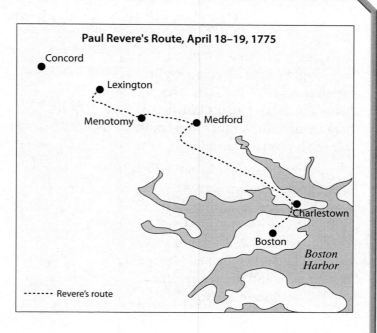

1. What town did Paul Revere ride through on his way from Boston to Lexington?

    a. Watertown

    b. Menotomy

    c. Lincoln

    d. Cambridge

2. Where was the first shot fired? Mark it on the map.

    a. Concord

    b. Boston

    c. Lexington

    d. Charlestown

3. What did the British expect to find at Concord?

    a. guns and ammunition

    b. Walden Pond

    c. horses and cattle

    d. North Bridge

Name: _____ **Date:** _____

Geography

Directions: Read the text, study the map, and answer the questions.

Battles of the American Revolution

The American Revolution was fought in the 13 colonies. It lasted from 1776 to 1783. The British hired German soldiers to help them fight. France and Spain joined the American side.

An important battle happened at Saratoga. The Americans won that battle. Fighting then shifted to the southern states. Yorktown was the last major battle. The French helped George Washington and the Americans win the battle and the war!

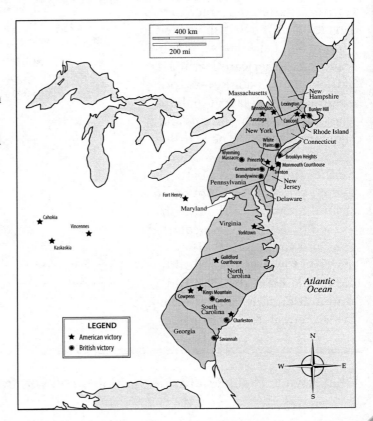

1. What country provided Britain with soldiers?

   a. France
   b. Spain
   c. Germany
   d. Canada

2. Where was the most southern battle fought?

   a. Charleston
   b. Lexington
   c. Cowpens
   d. Savannah

3. Look at the map. What were the four American victories outside the colonies?

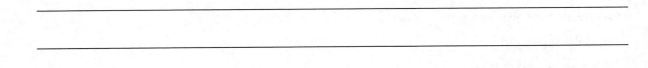

_____

_____

_____

Name: _____ **Date:** _____

Directions: Study the map, and answer the questions.

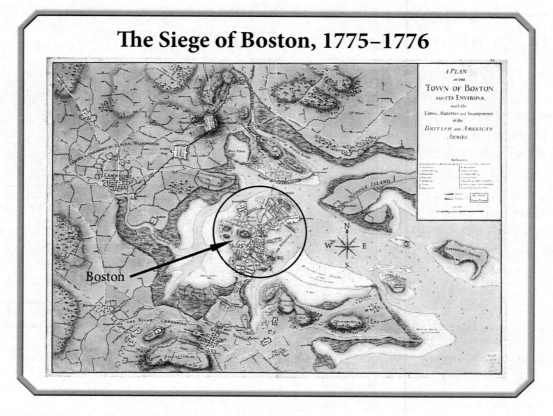

The Siege of Boston, 1775–1776

Boston

1. Which phrase best describes the location of Boston?

   a. almost surrounded by water   **c.** in a mountain region

   b. located inland   **d.** an island completely surrounded by water

2. The British had a powerful navy and lots of ships. Based on the map, why do you think it was not difficult for them to capture Boston?

   _____

   _____

   _____

3. What is east of Boston? Circle all that apply.

   a. mountains

   b. water

   c. Noddle Island

   d. forests

Name: _____ **Date:** _____

Geography

Directions: Study the map, and answer the questions.

The Battle of Yorktown

Yorktown was the war's last battle. American forces surrounded the British. George Washington led an army of soldiers and militiamen. French soldiers and their navy helped, too.

The British leader was Lord Charles Cornwallis. He had fewer troops. Some of them were German. The two sides fought. On October 19, 1781, the British waved the white flag. They surrendered.

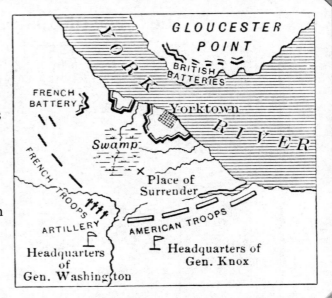

1. Notice where Washington set up his headquarters. Why is that specific place good?

   a. The high ground overlooks the British.

   b. It is close to the French and American armies.

   c. The place is a safe position for a leader.

   d. all the above

2. Pretend that you are General Washington directing your armies. Using the map, describe how you plan to defeat the British.

   _____

   _____

   _____

3. The British lost the battle and lost the war. When you lose a game, how do you react?

   _____

   _____

   _____

Name: _____ **Date:** _____

Directions: Compare the flags, and complete the Venn diagram.

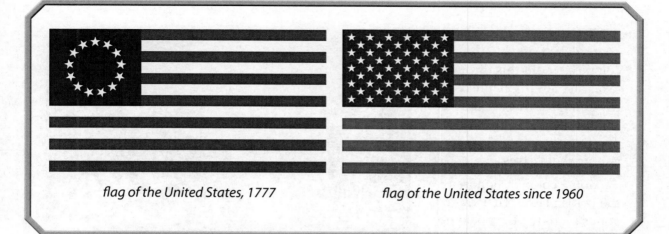

flag of the United States, 1777   flag of the United States since 1960

Then   **Now**

Economics

Name: _____ **Date:** _____

Directions: Read the text, and answer the questions.

Britain controlled how goods were traded in the colonies. It did this through taxes and laws. Colonists felt unhappy. They could not choose their trading partners. The colonies couldn't trade among themselves.

Some colonists ignored the British laws. They traded goods secretly. They paid no taxes on goods. These traders were smugglers. A lot of smuggling took place during the American Revolution.

1. What activity was against the law?
   a. shipping goods to Britain
   b. trading goods in secret
   c. trading goods with Britain
   d. buying goods from Britain

2. Who decided how the colonies should trade?
   a. merchants
   b. ship captains
   c. Britain
   d. the 13 colonies

3. How would smuggling hurt the British economy?
   a. Smugglers paid no taxes on goods.
   b. Traders couldn't choose their partners.
   c. Smuggling made trading dangerous.
   d. Smuggling relied on fast ships.

Name: _____ **Date:** _____

Directions: Read the text, and look at the images. Answer the questions.

Colonists used both paper money and coins. The paper money was counted in pounds, shillings, and pence. It was also used in Britain. Before the revolution, the coins used were mainly Spanish. Sometimes, colonists traded items instead of using cash. Eventually, each colony began to print its own paper money. This money was used to pay taxes to Britain.

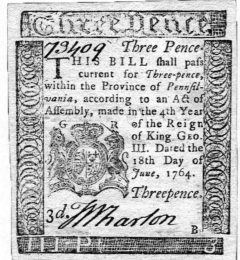

colonial paper money

1. Look at the images. Where was this money issued?

   a. the United States

   b. Britain

   c. Pennsylvania

   d. Massachusetts

2. What was used to produce this money?

   a. paper

   b. tin

   c. copper

   d. silver

3. Who was a printer of the money?

   a. King George III

   b. Benjamin Franklin

   c. Three-pence

   d. Province

Name:_____ **Date:**_____

Directions: Study the timeline, and answer the questions.

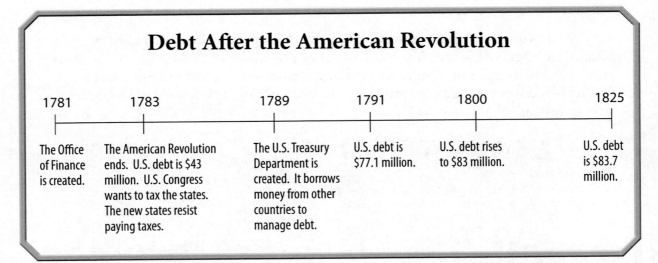

Debt After the American Revolution

1781	1783	1789	1791	1800	1825
The Office of Finance is created.	The American Revolution ends. U.S. debt is $43 million. U.S. Congress wants to tax the states. The new states resist paying taxes.	The U.S. Treasury Department is created. It borrows money from other countries to manage debt.	U.S. debt is $77.1 million.	U.S. debt rises to $83 million.	U.S. debt is $83.7 million.

Economics

1. Based on this timeline, when did national debt rise the most?

   a. between 1800 and 1825

   b. between 1791 and 1800

   c. between 1783 and 1791

   d. between 1791 and 1825

2. How did the U.S. government try to deal with the debt?

   a. raising taxes

   b. borrowing money

   c. waiting for money

   d. declaring bankruptcy

3. Why was it hard to pay off debt from the American Revolution?

   _____

   _____

   _____

   _____

   _____

   _____

Name: _____ **Date:** _____

Directions: Read the chart, and look at the images. Answer the questions.

The Coinage Act of 1792	
Eagles	$10.00
Half Eagles	$5.00
Quarter Eagles	$2.50
Dollars	$1.00
Half Dollars	$0.50
Quarter Dollars	$0.25
Dismes	$0.10
Half Dismes	$ 0.5
Cents	$.0.01
Half Cents	$0.005

The Coinage Act authorized the coins in the chart to be made. It gave people a common way to pay for goods and services. The coins below show images of Liberty and the American eagle. They also give the year of production.

1. How did making coins help Americans?

    a. They had one way to pay everywhere.

    b. They were free and safe.

    c. They didn't want to carry the money.

    d. They learned about fractions.

2. What were four kinds of coins, lowest to highest?

    a. half cents, dollars, dismes, eagles

    b. dollars, quarter eagles, half eagles, eagles

    c. cents, dismes, dollars, eagles

    d. dollars, half cents, half dismes, dismes

3. In 1792, all U.S. money was in coins. Now, some U.S. money is made of paper. Which do you prefer to use? Why?

    _____

    _____

    _____

Economics

Name: _____ **Date:** _____

Directions: Look at the images, and answer the question.

early American coins

modern money

1. Compare modern money to early American coins. How does American money show its history? How does it show what people believe?

_____

_____

_____

_____

_____

_____

Name: _____ **Date:** _____

Directions: Read the text, and answer the questions.

> The Founding Fathers were leaders from the 13 colonies. They met to make important decisions. They came from different walks of life. Some were lawyers. Some were merchants. George Washington and Benjamin Franklin were self-taught. Many of the men had gone to colonial colleges.
>
> These men led the colonies through a revolution. They united the country. The colonies broke away from Britain. The men then governed the new United States. In 1789, Washington was elected as the first U.S. president.

the Founding Fathers

History

1. Why are some colonists known as "the Founding Fathers"?

   a. They led the 13 colonies into one united country.

   b. They were all men with building experience.

   c. They were all men who started colonies.

   d. They found they agreed on many matters.

2. What things did the Founding Fathers do? Circle all that apply.

   a. They were leaders from the 13 colonies.

   b. They made important decisions.

   c. They were leaders during the revolution.

   d. all the above

3. What happened when the colonies broke away from Britain?

   _____

   _____

History

Name:_____ Date:_____

Directions: Read the text , and answer the questions.

> James Madison wrote well. He used his skill to help the new American government. He drafted the Constitution of the United States. He also drafted the Bill of Rights. Madison became known as the Father of the Constitution.
>
> Madison helped other Founding Fathers, such as George Washington. They set up the federal government. He supported Thomas Jefferson, too. Jefferson made a huge land deal. The Louisiana Purchase doubled the country's size.

Madison

Jefferson

Washington

1. What did Madison help Jefferson do?

   a. set up the new federal government

   b. buy more land for the United States

   c. pass laws for the United States

   d. write the U.S. Constitution

2. Based on the text, which of Madison's strengths was especially useful to the new country?

   a. talking in court

   b. encouraging others

   c. writing clearly

   d. making a deal

3. Based on the text, what is Madison considered the father of?

   a. his country

   b. his children

   c. the Louisiana Purchase

   d. the U.S. Constitution

Name: _____ Date: _____

Directions: Read the chart, and answer the questions.

History

Founding Fathers and Slavery

Slaveholders		Non-slaveholders	
Founding Father	Colony	Founding Father	Colony
John Hancock	Massachusetts	John Adams	Massachusetts
Charles Carroll	Maryland	Samuel Adams	Massachusetts
Samuel Chase	Maryland	Robert Treat Paine	Massachusetts
John Jay	New York	Roger Sherman	Connecticut
Benjamin Franklin	Pennsylvania	Oliver Ellsworth	Connecticut
Benjamin Rush	Pennsylvania	Alexander Hamilton	New York
Button Gwinnett	Georgia	Thomas Paine	Pennsylvania
Patrick Henry	Virginia		
Thomas Jefferson	Virginia		
Richard Henry Lee	Virginia		
James Madison	Virginia		
George Washington	Virginia		
Charles Cotesworth Pinckney	South Carolina		
Edward Rutledge	South Carolina		

1. Based on the chart, which colony had the most slaveholding Founding Fathers?

   a. South Carolina   **c.** Massachusetts

   b. Maryland   **d.** Virginia

2. Which colonies had both slaveholding and non-slaveholding Founding Fathers?

   a. Massachusetts, Connecticut, Maryland   **c.** New York, Massachusetts, Pennsylvania

   b. Pennsylvania, Maryland, Massachusetts   **d.** Connecticut, New York, Massachusetts

3. The slaveholding Founding Fathers outnumbered the non-slaveholding Founding Fathers. What does this tell you about slavery in the colonies?

   _____

   _____

   _____

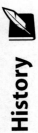

History

Name:_____ Date:_____

Directions: Read the text, and look at the image. Answer the questions.

The first Fugitive Slave Act was passed in 1793. The act gave slave owners the right to capture runaway slaves. It also said that children of enslaved women were slaves for life.

Slave catchers would also kidnap free black people. They brought them to slave states for money. People in the free states objected to this. They warned black people to be careful. They passed personal liberty laws. The laws gave people caught as slaves the right to trials.

A slave catcher closes in on a runaway slave.

1. What laws protected people taken as slaves?
   a. Fugitive Slave Act
   b. free slave laws
   c. personal liberty laws
   d. Runaway Slave Act

2. What did the Fugitive Slave Act permit slave catchers to do?

   _____

   _____

   _____

3. Slavery was a terrible time in U.S. history. What questions do you have about slavery?

   _____

   _____

   _____

Name: _____ **Date:** _____

Directions: Read the text, and look at the images. Answer the question.

This bell in Philadelphia has become a symbol of American freedom. The first bell from Britain cracked. It was melted down and replaced. That bell also cracked.

The inscription on the bell says "Proclaim LIBERTY Throughout all the Land unto all the Inhabitants Thereof."

1. The words on the Liberty Bell mean different things for different people. How would the Founding Fathers understand the words on the bell? How would an African American person in the early 1800s feel about the words on the bell?

_____

_____

_____

_____

_____

_____

_____

_____

_____

_____

Civics

Name: _____   Date: _____

Directions: Read the chart, and answer the questions.

Constitutional Powers		
Federal Powers	**Shared Powers (Federal and State)**	**State Powers**
• collect taxes • control trade • print money • establish post offices • protect patents and copyrights • set weights and measures • support the armed forces • set up federal courts • declare war • sign peace treaties • regulate immigration	• collect taxes • regulate drivers' licenses • set public school policies • build highways • set up courts • charter banks and corporations	• establish local governments • issue licenses • pass marriage and divorce laws • make business laws • conduct elections • approve changes to the U.S. Constitution • provide for public health and safety • build and maintain public schools

1. What does the federal government NOT control?

   a. printing of money

   b. how immigration is handled

   c. founding of post offices

   d. passing of marriage and divorce laws

2. Which power does both federal and state governments have?

   a. the setting of weights and measures

   b. the upkeep of public schools

   c. the signing of peace treaties

   d. the making of public school policies

3. What federal government activities deal with the economy? Circle all that apply.

   a. printing money

   b. signing peace treaties

   c. controlling trade

   d. regulating immigration

Name: _____ Date: _____

Directions: Read the chart, and answer the questions.

Key Changes to the U.S. Constitution	
Date	**Amendments**
1791	The first 10 amendments form the Bill of Rights. These protect people's freedoms. The amendments made changes to the Constitution.
1865	13th Amendment ends slavery.
1868	14th Amendment makes anyone born or living for a time in the United States a citizen.
1870	15th Amendment grants voting rights to all male citizens. Race and color do not matter.
1913	16th Amendment gives the federal government the right to collect taxes.
1920	19th Amendment gives women the right to vote.
1961	22nd Amendment limits U.S. presidents to two four-year terms.
1961	23rd Amendment lets the citizens of Washington, D.C., vote in the presidential election.
1971	26th Amendment lowers the voting age to 18.

march in Washington demanding the vote for women, 1913

1. In what year did women gain the right to vote?
    a. 1870
    b. 1920
    c. 1964
    d. 1971

2. In what year did slavery become illegal?
    a. 1861
    b. 1868
    c. 1865
    d. 1870

3. What is a constitutional amendment?
    a. a change to the Constitution
    b. a major new law about human rights
    c. an improvement in behavior
    d. a numbered part of the Constitution

Name: _____ Date: _____

Civics

Directions: Read the chart, and answer the questions.

The First 10 Amendments	
1st Amendment	It protects different kinds of freedom—freedom of religion, of speech, of the press, of peaceful assembly. It lets people's beliefs and ideas be heard.
2nd Amendment	Americans can bear arms.
3rd Amendment	Citizens do not have to shelter soldiers in their homes.
4th Amendment	Searches of a person's property cannot be unfair.
5th Amendment	Americans have the right to a fair and legal trial. They do not have to talk against themselves under oath. No one can be tried for the same crime twice.
6th Amendment	Americans should get a speedy trial.
7th Amendment	Americans have the right to trial by jury.
8th Amendment	Bail and fines cannot be too high. Punishment cannot be cruel and unusual.
9th Amendment	Not all rights are listed in the Constitution.
10th Amendment	If the Constitution has not given a power to the U.S. government, the power goes to the states or the people.

1. Which amendment protects you at a trial?

    a. the 1st amendment   **c.** the 5th amendment

    b. the 2nd amendment   **d.** the 9th amendment

2. You do not want a pipeline built. What amendment would support the right of your group to gather and protest?

    a. the 1st amendment

    b. the 2nd amendment

    c. the 3rd amendment

    d. the 4th amendment

3. What freedoms do you have because of the 1st amendment? Explain.

    _____

    _____

    _____

    _____

122

Name:_____ **Date:**_____

Directions: Read the text, and answer the questions.

Americans have rights, but they also fulfill duties as citizens. They are expected to obey federal, state, and local laws. They are required to pay taxes. Everyone pays sales tax when buying items. A citizen may have to do jury duty or be a witness in court. State laws demand that Americans attend school.

Adults are expected to vote in all elections. They need to keep informed about country, state, and local events. It is good to volunteer. There are many ways to help others.

 Theodore Roosevelt was the American president from 1901 to 1909. In 1883, when he was 25, he wrote an article titled *The Duties of American Citizenship.* Here are some of his ideas:

- To be a good citizen, you must be a good person.
- All citizens should take part in politics.
- Anyone who doesn't, shouldn't get the benefits of citizenship.
- Citizens must make sure that their governments act responsibly.
- It is also important for citizens to engage in community life.

1. What is an American duty? Based on the text, circle the best answer.

    a. volunteering

    b. helping others

    c. paying taxes

    d. showing respect

2. What did Theodore Roosevelt believe made a good citizen?

    _____

    _____

    _____

3. What can you do as a volunteer in your school?

    _____

    _____

    _____

Name: _____ **Date:** _____

Civics

Directions: Read the text, and design a poster.

> It was September 17, 1787, in Philadelphia, Pennsylvania. The delegates to the Constitutional Convention had an important role to play. They had to sign the Constitution of the United States.
>
> Since 2004, September 17 has been known as Constitution Day. It is a federal holiday for Americans. It is also known as "Citizenship Day."

1. Design a poster for a Constitution Day celebration in your community. Give the date, location, special events, and names of possible performers. Be sure to use patriotic colors and symbols in your design.

51397—180 Days of Social Studies

© *Shell Education*

Name: _____ Date: _____

Directions: Read the text, and study the image and map. Answer the questions.

Charles Mason and Jeremiah Dixon surveyed land. Their job was to define where one colony ended and the next began. They also set a north-to-south border. The survey took them four years. The Mason-Dixon line divided the North from the South.

1. What was the purpose of Mason and Dixon's work?

   a. to chart new roads

   b. to mark colony borders

   c. to map rivers and hills

   d. to sketch landmarks

2. Where is the longest part of the Mason-Dixon Line?

   a. between Pennsylvania and Maryland

   b. between West Virginia and Maryland

   c. between Delaware and Pennsylvania

   d. between Pennsylvania and West Virginia

3. What important division did the Mason-Dixon Line represent?

   a. Dutch colonies from British colonies

   b. East from West

   c. land colonies from water colonies

   d. North from South

Name: _____ **Date:** _____

Geography

Directions: Read the text, and answer the questions.

The Northwest Territory, 1787

Americans wanted to move west. Leaders in the new federal government knew this. They named the land south of the Great Lakes the Northwest Territory. In 1787, the Northwest Ordinance was passed. This law provided a way to create new states.

Over time, this area became six states: Ohio (1803), Indiana (1816), Illinois (1818), Michigan (1837), Wisconsin (1848), and Minnesota (1858).

1. What was the Northwest Territory's western boundary?

   a. Kentucky

   b. Louisiana

   c. Great Lakes

   d. Pennsylvania

2. Which rivers flowed into the Northwest Territory? Circle all that apply.

   a. the Ohio

   b. the Kentucky

   c. the Mississippi

   d. the St. Lawrence

3. Why did the federal government plan for future states?

   a. It expected settlers to go west.

   b. The country had states, not colonies.

   c. It was good at thinking ahead.

   d. The flag needed more stars and stripes.

Name: _____ **Date:** _____

Directions: Study the images, and answer the questions.

Enslaved black people worked on plantations. They were forced to work very long days. They could not freely leave the plantations. They had to follow many rules.

picking cotton

working in tobacco field

1. How were the enslaved people treated?

   a. They were working hard.

   b. They were watched.

   c. They got help with their work.

   d. They missed their homes.

2. Large plantations needed many people to grow crops. What kind of work was required?

   _____

   _____

   _____

3. What was life like for the enslaved people on plantations?

   _____

   _____

   _____

© Shell Education

Name: _____ **Date:** _____

Directions: Study the map, and answer the questions.

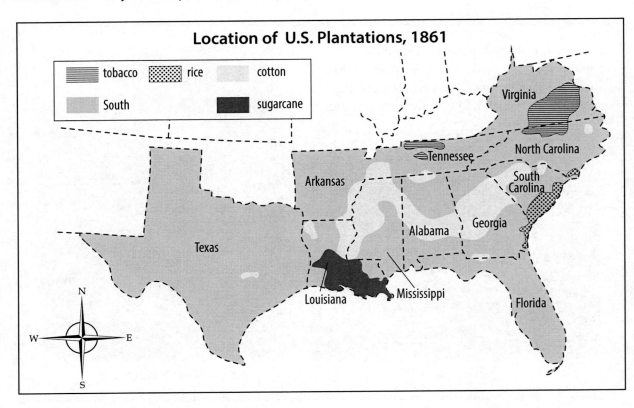

Location of U.S. Plantations, 1861

1. Where were most of the plantations located in the United States?

   a. Northwest

   c. Northeast

   b. Southwest

   d. Southeast

2. What do you notice about Alabama and Georgia?

   _____

   _____

   _____

3. Use evidence from the map to describe why most enslaved people lived in the South.

   _____

   _____

   _____

Name: _____ **Date:** _____

Directions: Read the text, and answer the questions.

The Jay Treaty helped the United States and Britain get along better. It solved some issues left over from the American Revolution.

- Britain would give up its forts in the Northwest Territory.
- Britain told its American Indian supporters not to attack the settlers there.
- Britain paid for 250 American ships it had taken.
- Britain agreed to trade with the United States.
- Both countries agreed on a United States–Canada border.
- The United States agreed not to help France fight Britain.
- The United States paid its debts from the revolution.

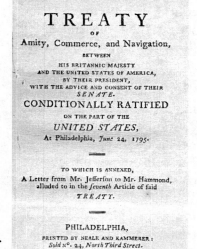

Geography

1. How did the treaty benefit both the United States and Britain? Use the Venn diagram to show your answer.

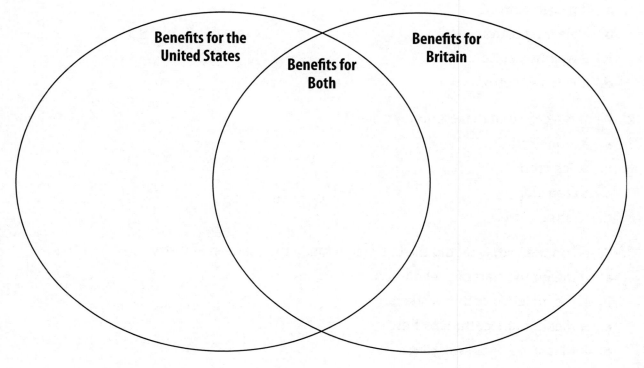

Benefits for the United States | Benefits for Both | Benefits for Britain

Economics

Name: _____ **Date:** _____

Directions: Read the text, and answer the questions.

Eli Whitney invented the cotton gin. His machine separated cotton fibers from seeds. Cotton could be processed more quickly. There was more than enough clean cotton. Cotton made farmers rich. Cotton became a cash crop. The cotton gin was the start of the Industrial Revolution in America.

Whitney charged the farmers a lot of money to use his cotton gins. Other people built copies. Farmers bought these cheaper machines. Whitney got a patent for his machine. This protected his idea.

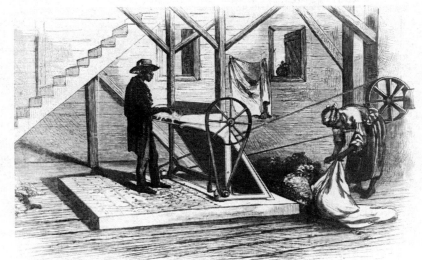

enslaved people working with a cotton gin

1. What did the cotton gin do well?
   a. It picked cotton.
   b. It cleaned cotton.
   c. It weighed cotton.
   d. It watered cotton.

2. What is a crop that makes money called?
   a. a money crop
   b. a rich crop
   c. a cash crop
   d. a farmer's crop

3. Based on the text, what did the cotton gin mean to American industry?
   a. It meant the start of a revolution.
   b. It meant fewer cotton workers.
   c. It meant more cotton clothes.
   d. It meant well-paid workers.

Name: _____ Date: _____

Directions: Read the text, and answer the questions.

Grinding wheat into flour is known as milling. In the old days, it took a lot of people to make flour. A better, cheaper way was needed.

In the 1780s, Oliver Evans designed a better mill. It made grinding wheat faster and cheaper. A waterwheel ran the mill. One man would empty the bags of wheat at one end. A second man would roll away barrels of flour at the other end. George Washington had Evans install an automated mill at Mount Vernon.

Evans kept improving his design. People built mills using his ideas. Evans earned money from the sales on his design.

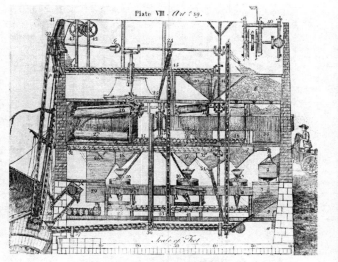

plan for the automated mill

1. How did Evans make money?
   a. He managed the crews that built automated mills.
   b. He milled flour at mills that adopted his design.
   c. He sold his mill design.
   d. He sold flour produced at his mills.

2. How did millers learn to build the automated mill?
   a. They hired Evans to help them build the mill.
   b. They studied a design Evans created.
   c. They visited a model mill at Mount Vernon.
   d. They attended classes at colonial colleges.

3. Why was it important to have a faster way to create flour?

   _____

   _____

   _____

Economics

Name: _____ **Date:** _____

Directions: Look at the picture, and answer the questions.

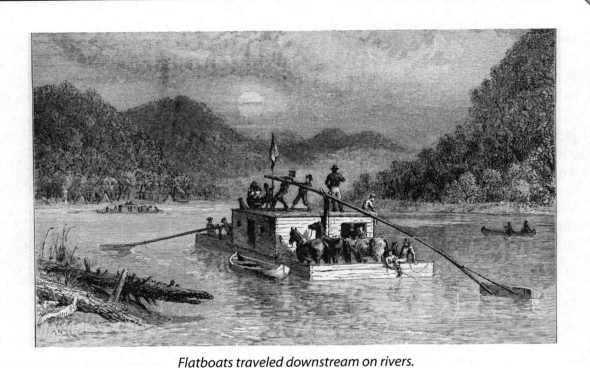

Flatboats traveled downstream on rivers.

1. Where did flatboats travel?

   a. upstream on lakes

   b. downstream on rivers

   c. on ocean currents

   d. upstream on rivers

2. What kinds of things did flatboats carry?

   _____

   _____

   _____

3. Flatboats could make only one-way trips. When they reached their destinations, their wood was sold. Why do you think that was?

   _____

   _____

   _____

Name: _____ **Date:** _____

Directions: Read the text, and answer the questions.

Samuel Slater wanted to move to America from Britain. He worked in a British cotton mill. British law refused to let textile workers go to America. Slater went anyway.

Slater knew how to make cotton-spinning machines. He built a cotton mill in Rhode Island in 1793. Soon, the country had many more mills. By 1850, there were over 1,000 cotton mills in the United States. Waterpower ran them. Young women worked in them. Children worked in them, too. Slater was called the "Founder of the American Industrial Revolution."

young people at a cotton-spinning machine

Economics

1. What two things did cotton mills need to run them?
   a. machines
   b. waterpower
   c. Samuel Slater
   d. farmers

2. What did Slater do for America?

   _____

   _____

   _____

3. Children used to work in mills. What jobs do you do at home and around the community?

   _____

   _____

   _____

   _____

Economics

Name: _____ Date: _____

Directions: Look at the images, and answer the question.

The farmer plowed the field, and then planted the seeds by hand.

The drill plow planted the seed and covered it at the same time.

1. Inventions in farming helped farmers produce more food. Describe why a farmer would have wanted to use the drill plow rather than the single plow.

_____

_____

_____

_____

_____

_____

134

© *Shell Education*

Name: _____ **Date:** _____

Directions: Read the text, and answer the questions.

The British were fighting France (1803–1815). They needed men to help them fight the war. They kidnapped American sailors. They forced them to work in their navy. The British also stopped American ships from going to France. Americans could not trade with France.

The British gave American Indians weapons. The American Indians wanted to keep their lands. They used the weapons to attack settlements.

In 1812, war broke out. The Americans and British, fought for nearly three years.

British forcing Americans into the Royal Navy

1. Why did the British seize American sailors?

   a. to work on British ships

   b. to tell British sailors what to do

   c. to help them trade with France

   d. to take weapons to the American Indians

2. Why did American Indians raid settlements?

   a. to get cattle and horses

   b. to protect their land

   c. to help the British army

   d. to trade with the settlers

3. The War of 1812 had several causes. Based on the text, what were two of the leading causes?

   a. British support of American Indian needs

   b. American anger at British taxes

   c. British taking of American sailors

   d. British making Americans work on farms

Name:_____ **Date:**_____

History

Directions: Read the text , and answer the questions.

It was 1815. The War of 1812 was over. The Treaty of Ghent was signed. Together, Americans had defended their country's interests. They felt a growing sense of unity. Some Americans were happy.

Neither the British nor the Americans had gained any land. The American Indians, however, had suffered loss. The treaty said they could keep their lands, but Americans ignored this. They settled on American Indian lands. As for enslaved Americans, the British had freed some of them during the war. Yet many people remained enslaved.

the end of the War of 1812

1. Many people were affected by the War of 1812. Which statement is NOT true?

   a. Some Americans were happy.

   b. Some enslaved people gained freedom.

   c. American Indians lost land to settlers.

   d. American Indians kept their lands.

2. Based on the text, why were some Americans happy? Circle all that apply.

   a. The War of 1812 was over.

   b. Americans did not lose any land.

   c. Americans had worked together during the war.

   d. Some enslaved people had gained freedom.

3. What national mood is caught in this 1819 painting? Circle all that apply.

   a. joy   **c.** confidence

   b. stress   **d.** pride

Name:_____ Date:_____

Directions: Read the chart, and answer the questions.

	Thomas Jefferson: Dreamer	
Years	**Role**	**Dream or Action**
late 1700s	colonist	dreamed of providing public education
1797–1801	U.S. vice president	building a public university
1801–1809	U.S. president	a university as more of a village than a house
1809–1817	retired citizen living in Virginia	shared his dream for public education with citizens and leaders sold his private library of 6,000 books to the Library of Congress to help rebuild the national library, which was burned in the War of 1812
1817–1825		construction of the buildings for the university using Jefferson's designs
1825	first dean of University of Virginia	opened the University of Virginia

1. After the War of 1812, how did Jefferson help his country rebuild?

   a. He sold his books to the national library.

   b. He served a term as U.S. president.

   c. He joined a lot of committees.

   d. He did a lot of daydreaming.

2. Based on the chart, what dream did Jefferson make a reality?

   a. offering public education

   b. building a university

   c. helping his country

   d. relaxing and reading books

3. After the War of 1812, many Americans felt confident and positive. How did Jefferson show that he was happy and hopeful? Explain.

   _____

   _____

   _____

Name: _____ **Date:** _____

History

Directions: Read the text, and look at the map. Answer the questions.

The Trail of Tears

After the War of 1812, more settlers moved west. They wanted to live and build on land that belonged to American Indians. Many American Indian tribes lived in the Southeast. They wanted to remain on their land. Some Americans wanted to let them stay on their land. Other Americans wanted to make them move.

In 1830, the U.S. president signed the Indian Removal Act. Several tribes were forced to leave their homes and move west of the Mississippi River. Their removal is called the "Trail of Tears."

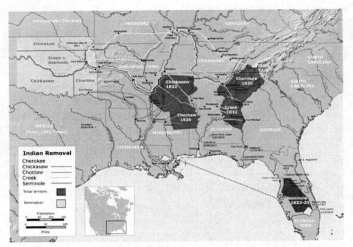

1. What would you have said to the president before he signed the Indian Removal Act?

_____

_____

_____

_____

_____

2. Why do you think this event is called the "Trail of Tears"?

_____

_____

_____

_____

_____

_____

51397—180 Days of Social Studies

© *Shell Education*

Name: _____ **Date:** _____

Directions: Read the text, and look at the map. Answer the question.

The War of 1812 was over. Americans felt confident. Many Americans headed west. American Indians were forced to move to make room. Some territories wanted to become states.

Missouri wanted to be like many Southern states. It wanted to be a slave state. But it was in the Midwest. Some groups wanted Missouri as a free state. Congress wanted to keep a balance between free and slave states. At the same time, Maine wanted to be a free state. The stalemate was over—Maine could be a free state, and Missouri could be a slave state. A bill was passed in 1820. It was called the "Missouri Compromise." Part of the compromise was that no other western territory could be a slave state.

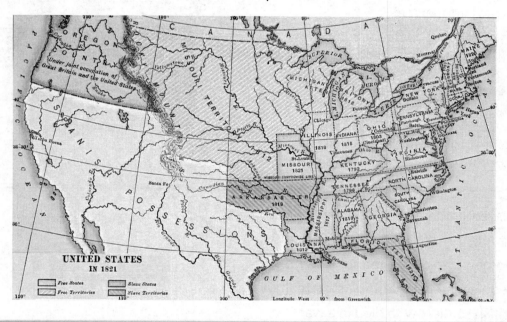

1. A compromise is an agreement where both sides give up something. Neither side is quite happy with the results. Why was the Missouri Compromise important?

_____

_____

_____

_____

_____

_____

Name: _____ Date: _____

Directions: Read the text, and answer the questions.

Americans have many national holidays. They honor events and people who helped make their country great. They build monuments about war.

On the last Monday in May, some Americans celebrate Memorial Day. On this day, they remember those who died while serving in the military. People visit cemeteries. They go to memorial services. They take part in parades.

They began to do this after the Civil War. The day was first called "Decoration Day." A group of women decorated the graves of soldiers. A group of freed slaves marched for those who had helped free them. Today, Memorial Day recognizes all members of the military—men and women—who died.

Memorial Day 1936

1. Who is remembered on Memorial Day?

    a. people freed from slavery after the Civil War

    b. women who decorated soldiers' graves

    c. people who died during active military service

    d. British soldiers who died in a war

2. Why was Memorial Day first known as "Decoration Day"?

    a. Soldiers who had earned medals had died.

    b. Everyone decorated their homes to celebrate.

    c. People decorated soldiers' graves.

    d. It was a law.

3. What is an example of a lasting memorial?

    a. flowers

    b. parades

    c. cakes

    d. monuments

Name: _____ **Date:** _____

Directions: Read the text, and answer the questions.

Veterans Day is November 11. It is a day for giving thanks to Americans who have served or now serve in the military. Its first name was "Armistice Day." *Armistice* means an agreement to stop fighting.

The day began after World War I ended. The treaty was signed in Paris. It was the eleventh hour of the eleventh day of the eleventh month. Over time, Americans fought in other wars, such as World War II and the Korean War. The day was renamed Veterans Day in 1954. On this day, people in the military are honored for their sacrifices for peace.

New York Tribune, *November 11, 1918*

1. Based on the text, who does Veterans Day honor?

   a. American veterans of World War I

   b. American veterans of World War II

   c. American veterans of the Korean War

   d. all the above

2. Why was November 11 chosen for Veterans Day?

   a. Americans need a holiday about then.

   b. World War I ended on that day.

   c. World War II ended on that day.

   d. Veterans chose the day by a vote.

3. Look at the front page of the newspaper. How does it show that the news is important?

   _____

   _____

   _____

Civics

Name: _____ **Date:** _____

Directions: Look at the image, and answer the questions.

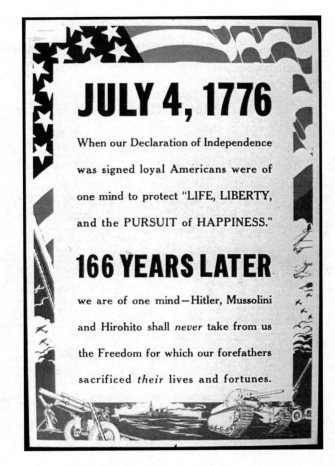

1. This poster repeats the phrase "of one mind." What does this phrase mean?

   a. to do one thing at a time
   b. to follow a leader's thinking
   c. to share a strong opinion
   d. to forget something

2. How does this poster use Independence Day to state something about world events?

   _____

   _____

3. You are planning an Independence Day party. Imagine that you can invite one or two people from American history to it. Who would they be? Explain your choices.

   _____

   _____

   _____

Name: _____ Date:_____

Directions: Read the text, look at the map, and answer the questions.

Christopher Columbus was an explorer. His goal was to find a water route to China. Instead, he found an unknown land. It was the "New World."

Columbus Day is currently a national holiday. It takes place in October. Some people celebrate it. They have parties and relax. Other people do not celebrate Columbus on this day. Instead, they honor American Indians. Columbus Day is known as "Indigenous People's Day" in some areas.

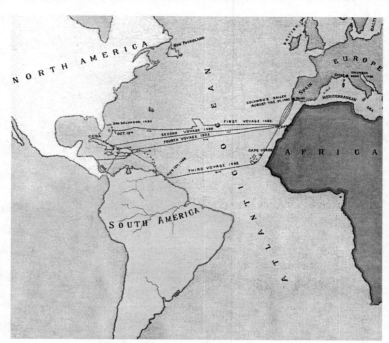

voyages of Columbus

1. Where did Christopher Columbus think he was headed?

   a. China

   b. Canada

   c. Chile

   d. Africa

2. What "New World" did Columbus discover for Spain? Circle all that apply.

   a. Central and South America

   b. the Caribbean

   c. Canada

   d. United States

3. Why do only some Americans celebrate this day? Do you celebrate it? Why?

   _____

   _____

   _____

   _____

Civics

Name: _____ **Date:** _____

Directions: Read the text, and answer the question.

Martin Luther King Jr. Day became a national holiday in 1983. It remembers the American civil rights leader and what he believed. King chose non-violent ways to make change. He organized marches. He gave speeches. He shared his dreams.

King was killed for his beliefs, but his dreams changed America.

I have a dream that one day this nation will rise up and live out the true meaning of its creed: "We hold these truths to be self-evident: that all men are created equal.

1. The words on the image come from a speech King gave in Washington, D.C. In your own words, explain his dream. How might you help make that dream happen?

_____

_____

_____

_____

_____

_____

_____

Name: _____ **Date:** _____

Directions: Read the text, and study the map. Answer the questions.

The United States was eager to claim more land and expand westward. In 1803, it purchased land from France. This was called the "Louisiana Purchase." The land extended from the Gulf of Mexico to what is now the Canadian border. As a result, the Americans controlled a new port—New Orleans. Farmers could take their goods there for trading. The land purchase included both sides of the Mississippi River. Some people called it "the deal of the century" because the land was so cheap.

1. The Louisiana Purchase included the land on the west side of which major river?

   a. Mississippi

   b. Columbia

   c. St. Lawrence

   d. Snake

2. Which port did the United States gain with this purchase?

   a. Oregon Country Port

   b. Columbia Port

   c. New Orleans Port

   d. San Francisco Port

3. Based on the map, which state was part of the Louisiana Purchase?

   a. Ohio

   b. Texas

   c. Mississippi

   d. South Dakota

Name: _____ **Date:** _____

Geography

Directions: Read the text, and answer the questions.

River systems became routes for travel and trade. Settlers wanted land along rivers. Rivers connected people to towns and villages. Traveling was easier on water than on land. Land trails went over rough ground. Rivers also provided drinking water. Keelboats, barges, and flatboats carried heavy items. Steamboats became a popular way to travel and greatly changed how people traveled on rivers.

Canals connected major lakes and waterways. They connected rivers to the Great Lakes. New York State built the Erie Canal. Canals also opened new ports for trade. Towns and cities were built at these ports. Canals connected northern and western America.

Cincinnati on the Ohio River, 1866

1. Why did settlers like to live close to water? Circle all that apply.
   a. Water allowed people to swim to town.
   b. Water was used for drinking, cooking, and chores.
   c. Water connected people to towns and villages.
   d. Water provided easy travel.

2. What did the canals connect? Circle all that apply.
   a. rivers to the Great Lakes
   b. northern territories to the West
   c. new ports for trade
   d. ocean ports

3. Based on the text, what kind of boat brought the greatest change to river travel?
   a. the flatboat
   b. the barge
   c. the keelboat
   d. the steamboat

Name: _____ **Date:** _____

Directions: Study the map, and answer the questions.

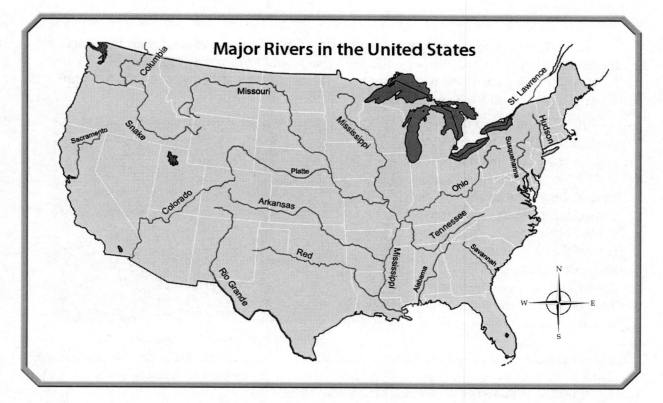

1. What long northwestern river flows into the Mississippi?

   a. Platte

   b. Missouri

   c. Columbia

   d. Snake

2. What river flows southeast along a major border?

   a. Ohio

   b. Sacramento

   c. Rio Grande

   d. Platte

3. What do you think is the most important American river? Why?

   _____

   _____

   _____

Name: _____ **Date:** _____

Directions: Read the text, and answer the questions.

In 1804, Americans were looking westward. They wanted to expand their influence there. Was there a passage through the West that would open more trade routes? The Lewis and Clark Expedition would find out. The explorers paddled west on the Missouri River. They traveled to the Pacific Ocean.

The trip was long and hard. American Indians, the military, and fur traders helped Lewis and Clark. They saw the Rocky Mountains. They pressed on and climbed over them. They arrived at the Pacific Ocean. They then returned east with their plant and animal samples. They drew many maps of the land. They opened a new route for Americans to settle in the West.

William Clark's signature on a rock

1. Based on the text, why did Lewis and Clark journey west?

   a. to expand American influence in the West

   b. to get animal and plant samples

   c. to find a passage through the West for a new route

   d. all the above

2. Who helped Lewis and Clark on their expedition? Circle all that apply.

   a. soldiers

   b. gold miners

   c. fur traders

   d. American Indians

3. Engravings on rocks have been found all over the world. Why do you think Clark put his name on a rock? What message would you carve into a rock? Why?

   _____

   _____

   _____

Name:_____ **Date:**_____

Directions: Read the text, and answer the question.

America was on the move. The Lewis and Clark Expedition had created much interest in what was called the "Oregon Country." Americans worked with the British to set a Pacific Northwest border. More land became part of the United States.

In the Southwest, Americans fought Mexico. After the war, Texas and other southwest areas became part of America. They also bought land from Mexico in 1853. This was called the "Gadsden Purchase." Between 1800 and 1853, the United States grew westward. From its 13 original colonies, it spread across North America to the Pacific Ocean.

battle of the Mexican-American War, 1846

1. In the 1800s, what did the United States do to grow in the west?

_____

_____

_____

_____

_____

_____

_____

_____

Name: _____ Date: _____

Economics

Directions: Read the text, and answer the questions.

The War of 1812 cost a lot of money. The country built ships, fed soldiers, and bought weapons. The United States was struggling to pay its debts. The government needed to collect taxes to pay what it owed.

After the war, settlers moved west. The new settlements became centers for pork and grain production. Soon, industry boomed, and taxes flowed.

The textile industry also grew. Factories in the North needed raw materials. This demand led to the growth of cotton production in the South. Slavery was important to the South's economy.

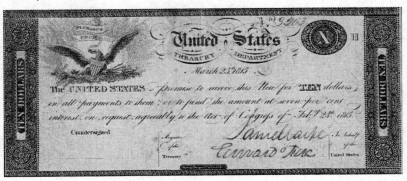

a U.S. treasury note

1. Why did the country need a strong economy when the war ended?
   a. They needed to feed the soldiers.
   b. There were big war debts to pay off.
   c. People wanted to get richer.
   d. The ships were no longer useful.

2. What did settlers produce in the northwest?
   a. pork and grain
   b. chickens and corn
   c. cotton
   d. bison

3. Based on the text, why was cotton production booming?
   a. Field workers got little pay.
   b. The war against Britain was over.
   c. Factories in the North needed cotton.
   d. American Indians traded goods for cotton.

Name: _____ **Date:** _____

Directions: Read the text, and answer the questions.

Economics

War debts were being paid off. Tax dollars came from industries such as textiles. Industry was growing in the North. Women worked but had fewer options than men. The textile factories needed many workers. Women worked well with textiles. Young women were hired to live and work there. They worked 10 to 12 hours a day. They sent most of what they earned to their families.

Not all women worked in factories. Enslaved women worked in the fields. They also worked in their owners' houses. They cleaned and cooked. They also raised children.

Some American Indian women prepared hides to trade with eastern explorers.

textile workers

1. Based on the text, in what industry did northern white women work?

   a. cotton

   b. pork

   c. shipping

   d. textiles

2. What jobs did enslaved women do? Circle all that apply.

   a. They did field work.

   b. They cooked and cleaned.

   c. They raised children.

   d. They made textiles.

3. Why do you think young women sent so much of their money to their families?

   _____

   _____

   _____

Economics

Name: _____ Date: _____

Directions: Look at the map, and read the text. Answer the questions.

The Treaty of Guadalupe Hidalgo, 1848

In 1845, President James K. Polk wanted to buy land from Mexico. Mexico refused to sell its land. War broke out. America won the war. In 1848, the two countries signed a treaty. Mexico gave up the land.

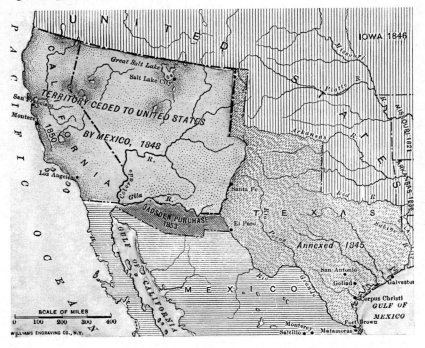

1. What country controlled California in 1847?

    a. Mexico

    b. England

    c. Spain

    d. America

2. Circle two words on the map that you don't know. Work with a partner to define the words.

    _____

    _____

    _____

Name: _____ **Date:** _____

Directions: Read the chart, and answer the questions.

Item	Cost in 1820s
1 cow	$12
1 acre of land	$2
1 pound of coffee	17¢
10 pounds of sugar	20¢

1. How much is the coin worth?

   a. half cent

   b. one cent

   c. 25 cents

   d. 10 cents

2. How many of these coins would you need to buy one pound of coffee?

   _____

   _____

3. Why do you think a cow costs more than an acre of land?

   _____

   _____

   _____

4. It is the 1820s. You own a general store. Based on the chart, how much would you charge for 5 pounds of coffee and 20 pounds of sugar? Explain.

   _____

   _____

   _____

Economics

Name: _____ **Date:** _____

Directions: Look at the images, and answer the question.

1. Why were women important to the American economy in the 1800s?

_____

_____

_____

_____

_____

_____

_____

_____

_____

Name:_____ Date:_____

Directions: Read the text, and answer the questions.

Americans began to go to Oregon Country. They hoped to gain good farmland. They had a sense of adventure.

In 1843, 1,000 people headed to Oregon Country. They used 100 covered wagons. They traveled with 5,000 cattle and oxen. The journey was 2,000 miles long. It was the Great Migration of 1843.

OREGON CITY.

Oregon City, 1850s (near current-day Portland)

History

1. Why did settlers move to Oregon Country?
   a. They wanted to trade with American Indians.
   b. They wanted better farmland.
   c. They wanted to be fur traders.
   d. The American president told them to move.

2. In one year, how many men, women, and children traveled to Oregon Country?
   a. 1,000
   b. 5,000
   c. 100
   d. 2,000

3. Why was the 1843 journey called the "Great Migration"?

_____

_____

_____

_____

_____

_____

History

Name:_____ Date:_____

Directions: Read the text, and answer the questions.

Settlers got ready carefully for their long trip on the Oregon Trail. They prepared food that would not spoil. Early settlers found that large wagons were too heavy. They got stuck in mud. Animals died from pulling them.

A light, sturdy covered wagon was created. It was called the prairie schooner. The small wagon looked like a sailboat floating over the Prairies. Oxen pulled it. They were strong and ate anything. Settlers filled the wagons with food and items such as furniture, dishes, and tools. Both men and women drove the wagons.

on the Oregon Trail

1. What were the benefits of pulling wagons with oxen? Circle the two best answers.

   a. They were fast.

   b. They ate anything.

   c. They were lazy.

   d. They were strong.

2. Why was the prairie schooner a good wagon for the trip? Circle the two best answers.

   a. It was light and could be pulled easily.

   b. Young children could drive it.

   c. People could ride in it because it was big.

   d. It was sturdy.

3. People often had to walk beside the wagons. Why would they do that?

   a. They liked to keep fit.

   b. There was no room inside.

   c. They enjoyed nature.

   d. Their leaders told them to.

Name: _____ **Date:** _____

Directions: Look at the images, and answer the questions.

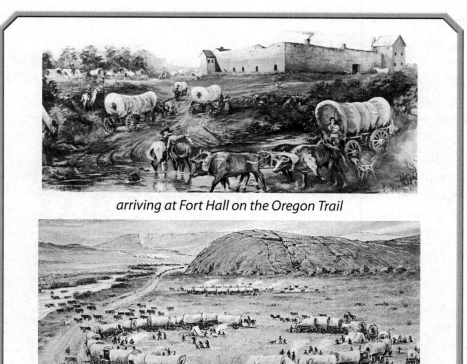

arriving at Fort Hall on the Oregon Trail

on the Oregon Trail

History

1. Why do you think settlers liked to camp close to forts?

_____

_____

_____

_____

2. Why do you think settlers might camp in a small circle formation rather than a big circle formation?

_____

_____

_____

_____

_____

History

Name: _____ Date: _____

Directions: Read the text, and answer the questions.

In fair weather, a wagon train could travel about 10 miles a day. In rainy weather, it moved more slowly. Children were expected to help. They cooked, helped drive the wagon, and guided cattle on horseback. Toddlers and babies were watched to keep them from harm. In some families, children wrote the family journal.

When the wagon train stopped for the night, everyone set up camp. After dinner, they sang and danced to lift their spirits. Children had very few toys. They made their own. They also collected items found along the trail.

By the late 1860s, fewer settlers took trails. The railroad made the trip west easier, cheaper, and faster.

making camp on the trail

1. What work did children do along the Oregon Trail?
   a. They cooked.
   b. They guided cattle on horseback.
   c. They drove the wagon.
   d. all the above

2. What did children do for entertainment along the Oregon Trail?
   a. sang and danced
   b. played catch
   c. rode the railroad
   d. cooked meals

3. How do you prefer to take a long trip?

   _____

   _____

   _____

Name: _____ **Date:** _____

Directions: Read the text, and look at the images. Answer the question.

On the Oregon Trail, setters shot bison. They burned firewood. Their oxen grazed on prairie grass. But they faced many hardship along the way. About 20,000 people died along the trail. Prairie fires, drownings, and bison stampedes killed people. Diseases and mountain fevers made them sick. Settlers feared attacks from American Indians. Instead, many settlers got help from them. American Indians rescued settlers from drowning. They pulled wagons from ruts and mud. They found lost cattle.

1. The settlers faced hardships along the Oregon Trail. They also brought hardships to American Indians. How do you think life along the trail changed?

_____

_____

_____

_____

_____

_____

_____

_____

_____

Civics

Name: _____ Date: _____

Directions: Read the text, and answer the questions.

James Monroe was the fifth president of the United States. He had a lot of land in Virginia. His plantation was called Highland. At one time, he had over 3500 acres. He owned slaves who worked on his large plantation.

During his life, he owned 250 slaves. However, he thought that slavery should end. In a letter in 1829, he said that slavery was "one of the evils still remaining" in the United States.

James Monroe

1. Where was James Monroe's plantation?
   a. Virginia
   b. Pennsylvania
   c. Washington
   d. Georgia

2. What did James Monroe think about slavery?
   a. that it was a good thing
   b. that it should end
   c. that it should remain in the South
   d. that it should remain for 50 more years

3. What do you think James Monroe meant by "one of the evils still remaining?"

   _____

   _____

   _____

Name: _____ Date: _____

Directions: Read the text, and answer the questions.

The Compromise of 1850 set boundaries for new territories. It identified free states and slave states. It also passed laws about slavery. One change was the Fugitive Slave Act. The law said that all runaway slaves should be returned to their owners. Anyone caught helping a runaway slave could be jailed and fined. This law was dangerous for free black men and women. They could be accused of being runaway slaves. Then, those free people could be enslaved.

At that time, the words of a free black man or woman held no power, but the words of a white person did. Harriet Beecher Stowe wanted slavery abolished. She also knew how to tell a moving story. Her book *Uncle Tom's Cabin* describes how enslaved people suffered. Many people read it.

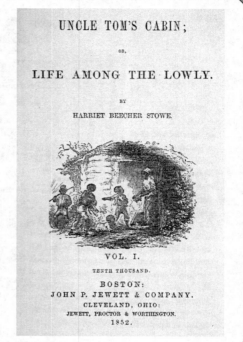

UNCLE TOM'S CABIN;

OR,

LIFE AMONG THE LOWLY.

BY

HARRIET BEECHER STOWE.

VOL. I.

TENTH THOUSAND.

BOSTON:
JOHN P. JEWETT & COMPANY.
CLEVELAND, OHIO:
JEWETT, PROCTOR & WORTHINGTON.
1852.

Civics

1. What did the Fugitive Slave Act expect people to do?
   a. return fugitives to their owners
   b. help fugitives escape
   c. send fugitives to the West
   d. help fugitives as needed

2. What might happen if a person let a fugitive stay free? Circle all that apply.
   a. The person could be fined.
   b. The person could be given an award.
   c. Nothing would happen to the person.
   d. The person could be put in jail.

3. Based on the text, how did Harriet Beecher Stowe protest against slavery?
   a. She wrote newspaper articles against it.
   b. She wrote a book about how slaves lived.
   c. She spoke about runaway slaves in court.
   d. She gave emotional speeches in Boston.

Civics

Name: _____ Date: _____

Directions: Read the poster, and answer the questions.

CAUTION!!

COLORED PEOPLE

OF BOSTON, ONE & ALL,

You are hereby respectfully CAUTIONED and advised, to avoid conversing with the

Watchmen and Police Officers of Boston,

For since the recent **ORDER OF THE MAYOR & ALDERMEN,** they are empowered to act as

KIDNAPPERS

AND

Slave Catchers,

And they have already been actually employed in **KIDNAPPING, CATCHING, AND KEEPING SLAVES.** Therefore, if you value your **LIBERTY,** and the *Welfare of the Fugitives* among you, *Shun* them in every possible manner, as so many *HOUNDS* on the track of the most unfortunate of your race.

Keep a Sharp Look Out for KIDNAPPERS, and have TOP EYE open.

APRIL 24, 1851.

1. Where and when was this poster written?

   a. Boston, 1851   **c.** Kansas, 1850

   b. Philadelphia, 1776   **d.** Boston, 1888

2. Who were people warned to be careful of? Circle all that apply.

   a. aldermen

   b. watchmen

   c. abolitionists

   d. police officers

3. Why was this poster written?

   _____

   _____

   _____

Name: _____ **Date:** _____

Directions: Read the text, and answer the questions.

> Whereas the Negroes in the counties of Bristol and Worcester, the 24th of March last, petitioned the Committees of Correspondence for the county of Worcester (then convened in Worcester) to assist them in obtaining their freedom.
>
> Therefore, in County Convention, June 14th, 1775
>
> Resolved, that we abhor the enslaving of any of the human race, and particularly of the Negroes in this country. And that whenever there shall be a door opened, or opportunity present for any thing to be done toward the emancipating the Negroes, we will use our influence and endeavor that such as thing may be effected. Attest, William Henshaw, Clerk.
>
> *This is a document written in 1775 about slavery.*

1. Why are the Committees of Correspondence being petitioned?
   a. to help enslaved people gain their freedom
   b. to be warned about slavery
   c. to help capture runaway slaves
   d. to assist people with opening doors

2. How do you think the people who wrote this document feel about slavery?"

   _____

   _____

   _____

   _____

   _____

   _____

Name:_____ Date:_____

Directions: Read the text, and answer the questions.

Civics

James Monroe was an anti-federalist. This group wanted to make laws for their own states. They were against a strong federal government. Federalists favored a strong national government. They wanted to make laws for everyone across the country. Generally, federalists were against slavery. Monroe was one of the few anti-federalists who was also against slavery.

As the United States spread westward, Congress and the Senate had many debates about free states and slave states. Should there be both? Who should decide? How? In the years before the Civil War, there was much debate on four ideas.

№ 1. Congress should stop the spread of slavery.

№ 2. Each state or territory should be able to be a free state or a slave state. The people who lived there should make the choice.

№ 3. Congress must protect the rights of all people. Slaves were property. Slave owners' rights must be protected.

№ 4. Slavery past the Missouri Compromise line is unlawful. This line should be pushed to the Pacific coast.

1. Which ideas are federalist? Which ideas are anti-federalist? Why do you think that? Explain.

_____

_____

_____

_____

_____

_____

_____

_____

51397—180 Days of Social Studies　　　　　　　　　　　　　© *Shell Education*

Name: _____ **Date:** _____

Directions: Read the text, and study the map. Answer the questions.

Fur traders and explorers began using the Oregon Trail in the early nineteenth century. They could travel only by foot or on horses. Then more people moved west. The trail had to be widened. Large wagons were able to travel on it. Settlers traveled from Missouri to Oregon.

The first group of settlers set out in covered wagons. These were known as wagon trains. They set out on the trail in the 1840s. Families wanted to build new farms. They found the trip hard. They left many things by the trail's side to lighten the wagons. The heavy wagons left wheel ruts that can still be seen.

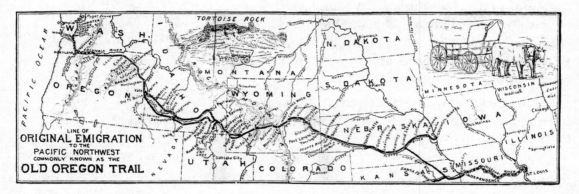

1. Based on the text, why was the Oregon Trail widened?

   a. to give more room to riders on horseback

   b. to enable farmers to make faster journeys

   c. to make way for big covered wagons

   d. to let people walk beside one another

2. Why did the settlers leave things beside the trail?

   a. They left them to help other travelers.

   b. They needed to make the wagons lighter.

   c. They needed to help mark the trail.

   d. Not littering was not important then.

3. What is a wagon train?

   a. a steam train carrying wooden wagons

   b. a group of people with movable homes

   c. the deep ruts left on western trails

   d. a line of covered wagons pulled by animals

Name: _____ Date: _____

Geography

Directions: Read the text, and answer the questions.

In 1848, James Wilson Marshall discovered gold in northern California. He found it in the river at Sutter's Mill. John Sutter tried to keep it a secret.

The news got out. About 300,000 people rushed to California. They came from all over the world. Most of them arrived in 1849. They were called the "forty-niners." This was the beginning of the Gold Rush. They found gold by washing gravel in pans. This was known as "panning." Later, they had to dig mines for gold. When the gold was gone, people moved on. The result was many ghost towns.

Other people stayed, and California grew. It became a state in 1850. The Gold Rush ended by 1855.

a gold miner on his way to California

1. How long did the Gold Rush last?

   a. 9 years

   b. 6 years

   c. 49 years

   d. 12 years

2. What caused the ghost towns?

   a. Many miners died when looking for gold.

   b. California welcomed many ghosts.

   c. People left when the gold was gone.

   d. California towns had limited lives.

3. Based on the text, why did so many people go to California?

   a. to visit the ghost towns

   b. to enjoy the good climate

   c. to join the great move west

   d. to look for gold

Name: _____ **Date:** _____

Directions: Study the map, read the text, and answer the questions.

The California Trail began in Missouri. In the 1840s, people found traveling on it hard. They had to cross deserts and mountains. Some of them died trying. Sometimes their wagons got stuck or broken. Sometimes cattle and horses wandered off or died.

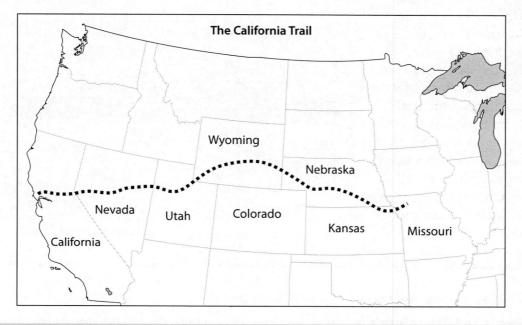

The California Trail

1. Based on the text, what are some of the hardships settlers faced on the trail? Circle all that apply.

   a. crossing deserts

   b. wagons getting stuck

   c. livestock dying

   d. getting lost

2. Which states did the settlers travel through on their way to California?

   _____

   _____

3. What do you think would have been the hardest part of traveling on a trail?

   _____

   _____

   _____

Geography

Name:_____ Date:_____

Directions: Read the text, and look at the map. Answer the questions.

In 1846, Mormons were driven out of Illinois. People there did not like their beliefs. Brigham Young led them west. The trip was hard. The weather was bad, and they were not well prepared. That trail became known as the "Mormon Trail." It was a 1,300-mile journey.

Mormons founded Salt Lake City, Utah. They set up their church there. For more than 20 years, other Mormons took the trail west. Poor settlers carried their goods in handcarts. Some who could not afford oxen pulled their own carts. Once the railroad was built, the trail wasn't used anymore.

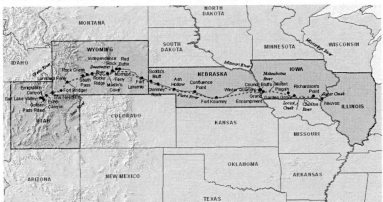

sites along the Mormon Trail

1. Why did Mormons head west? Circle all that apply.
   a. They needed a safe home.
   b. They searched for adventure.
   c. They wanted a trail of their own.
   d. They had to leave their first settlement.

2. Why did Mormons stop using the trail?
   a. The weather was always poor.
   b. Travel by train was easier.
   c. They had run out of wagons.
   d. They had done enough walking.

3. Why do you think the Mormons took such a long trip? If you were in their shoes, would you have gone so far?

   _____

   _____

   _____

   _____

Name:_____ **Date:**_____

Directions: Look at the images, and answer the question.

California Trail

Mormon Trail

1. Many trails were created across America. Explain why these trails were made.

_____

_____

_____

_____

_____

_____

Name: _____ Date: _____

Economics

Directions: Read the text, and answer the questions.

In the 1800s, factories needed many workers. The work was divided up. Each person did a small part of a bigger job. Factories often used machines to make the work simpler. Yet employees still worked long hours six days a week. Many women and children worked in factories. Working there was dangerous.

Textile factories produced cloth. Workers used sewing machines to make clothes. Workers had no control over the products. In the past, skilled workers had made products in small shops. They controlled what they made.

1. Based on the text, what did factory workers do? Circle all that apply.
   a. They had machines to help do the work.
   b. They each created finished products.
   c. They each did a certain part of a job.
   d. They all moved to Massachusetts.

2. What did factory owners do?
   a. They hired many workers.
   b. They shared their earnings with their employees.
   c. They made sure that their workers were safe.
   d. none of the above

3. Based on the text, what did workers in small shops do that factory workers didn't?
   a. They produced items more cheaply.
   b. They had a sense of ownership.
   c. They set their own times to work.
   d. They created whole items.

Economics

Name: _____ **Date:** _____

Directions: Look at the image, read the text, and answer the questions.

In the southern states, many farms grew tobacco, cotton, sugarcane, and rice to sell. These large farms were called "plantations." Harvesting these crops needed a lot of workers. Hiring workers was expensive. So, landowners decided to use enslaved people as free labor.

Most enslaved people worked in the fields. Some of them worked in their owners' houses. Slaves worked long hours. Their lives were harsh. Their houses were poor. However, many of the owners had grand houses.

plantation slave houses

1. What were plantations?
   a. large farms full of greenhouses
   b. large areas planted with trees
   c. southern homes for enslaved people
   d. large farms with crops to sell

2. Look at the image. Which statement is true about the slave houses?
   a. They were very large.
   b. They were well made.
   c. They were small and poorly made.
   d. They had no chimneys.

3. Owners and enslaved people both lived on plantations. How were their houses different?

   _____

   _____

   _____

Economics

Name: _____ Date: _____

Directions: Look at the map, and read the caption. Answer the questions.

Pony Express Route

The stations on the Pony Express were 10 miles apart.

1. Based on the number of stations, about how many miles of the route does this map represent?

   a. 160

   b. 280

   c. 190

   d. 375

2. Riders covered about 75 miles each day. How long would it take a rider from St. Joseph to reach Fort Kearny?

   a. three days

   b. four days

   c. five days

   d. four hours

3. What does the closeness of the horse-changing stations tell you about the kind of service that the Pony Express offered?

   _____

   _____

   _____

Name:_____   Date:_____

Directions: Read the text, and answer the questions.

In the 1800s, people found it hard to communicate with each other. Messages took a long time. They had to travel by horse, carriage, or ship.

In the 1830s, Samuel Morse invented the telegraph. He could send messages along wires strung along poles. He spelled words using short dots and long dashes. Trained operators would hear the dots and dashes and record the words. Morse code signals let people get in touch with each other over great distances. Morse's best-known code is SOS—three dots, three dashes, and three more dots. The distress signal is still used worldwide.

old telegraph machine

The telegraph helped the economy. Goods could be ordered across the country in minutes. People could find out quickly how much things cost in different parts of the United States. This was all thanks to the speed of messages over the telegraph.

1. What were the benefits of the telegraph?
   a. helping the economy
   b. communicating over long distances
   c. learning a common signal for distress
   d. all the above

2. What was important to have in order for telegraphs to work?
   a. cables
   b. ships
   c. trained staff
   d. flag signals

3. Describe your own special way to send messages to a friend?

   _____

   _____

   _____

Economics

Name: _____ Date: _____

Directions: Look at the images, and answer the question.

southern plantation

Boston, 1850s

1. Imagine you lived in the South in the nineteenth century. How would you tell a buyer in Boston about how much cotton you grew? List several ways. Explain.

_____

_____

_____

_____

_____

174

Name: _____ **Date:** _____

Directions: Read the text, and answer the questions.

The United States was not always united. The 11 Southern states did not want to stay within the country. They called themselves the "Confederate" states. The group wanted to govern itself. The Southern states wanted enslaved people to work in their cotton fields. Their wealth and way of life depended on this.

The Northern 22 states were known as the Union. They wanted to get rid of slavery. They wanted all people to live as free and independent humans.

The Civil War broke out in April 1861. A civil war is a fight between groups in the same country.

Confederate attack on Fort Sumter, April 12–13, 1861

History

1. Based on the text, why did states in the South want to leave the United States?
   a. It was a way to keep slavery illegal.
   b. The North and the South had little in common.
   c. They wanted to keep slavery.
   d. They were outnumbered by the Northern states.

2. Based on the text, why did Union states want to end slavery?
   a. to let the people work in northern factories
   b. to let the people live as independent humans
   c. to welcome more Southerners to the North
   d. to upset and disturb the Southern states

3. What is a civil war?
   a. a family war between brothers and sisters
   b. a long battle between good and evil
   c. a fight between people in the same country
   d. a war between rich and poor civilians

Name: _____ Date: _____

History

Directions: Read the text, and answer the questions.

In 1860, a man from the North was elected president of the United States. He was Abraham Lincoln. Very soon, seven Southern states *seceded* from the United States. This means they left the country. They were convinced that Lincoln would end slavery. People in the free states had voted for him. Civil war was not long off.

In 1863, Lincoln passed a law to free all American slaves. Later that year, he also made a famous speech—the Gettysburg Address. In it, Lincoln called for freedom and equality. It was a call for unity and for hope for the future.

———————— ☆ ————————

Four score and seven years ago our fathers brought forth on this continent, a new nation, conceived in Liberty, and dedicated to the proposition that all men are created equal.

———————— ☆ ————————

Abraham Lincoln, Nov. 19, 1863

1. Why did people in the North vote for Lincoln?
   a. He gave great short speeches.
   b. He believed that slavery should end.
   c. He was ready to start a civil war.
   d. He was a man from Kentucky.

2. What did the Southern states do after the election?
   a. They joined England.
   b. They stopped growing cotton.
   c. They left the United States.
   d. They moved west.

3. Look at the words from Lincoln's Gettysburg Address. How do his words relate to causes of the Civil War?

   _____

   _____

   _____

Name: _____ **Date:** _____

Directions: Study at the image, and answer the questions.

History

I AM NOT A MAN AND A BROTHER?

1. Abolitionists wanted to end slavery. Why did they create this image?

_____

_____

_____

_____

2. How do you think the image was meant to make people feel? Why?

_____

_____

_____

_____

_____

Name: _____ **Date:** _____

History

Directions: Read the text, and answer the questions.

The first shots of the Civil War were fired at Fort Sumter in South Carolina. Union soldiers defended the fort. The soldiers were low on supplies, including food. A supply ship was expected.

On April 12, 1861, the Confederate forces attacked. The two sides fought for 34 hours. The Battle of Fort Sumter ended when the Union soldiers gave up the fort. No one was killed. The Confederate win encouraged four more Southern states to leave the Union. The Civil War raged on for four more years.

Battle of Fort Sumter

1. What phrase best describes the Battle of Fort Sumter?
   a. first land battle of the Civil War
   b. first sea battle of the Civil War
   c. first Union win of the Civil War
   d. first long siege of the Civil War

2. Based on the location of the fort, why was this an easy target for the Confederate army to attack?

   _____

   _____

   _____

3. In the Civil War, Americans fought against each other. If you and another family member found yourselves on opposite sides of a conflict, how would you feel? What would you do?

   _____

   _____

   _____

Name: _____ **Date:** _____

Directions: Read the caption, and look at the image. Answer the question.

The United States was a divided country. People had different needs and beliefs in the North and the South. In 1861, they went to war.

1. What differences made the North and the South decide to fight each other?

_____

_____

_____

_____

_____

_____

_____

_____

_____

_____

_____

Name:_____ Date:_____

Civics

Directions: Read the text, look at the image, and answer the questions.

The 13 colonies broke away from Britain in 1776. Each colony had its own rules and laws. Then they became states. They didn't feel strong enough on their own. It was time to create a central government.

In 1789, the Constitution called for a united government. It granted many rights to Americans. The government was given the power to tax people. It could also require them to defend their country. But, states still made most decisions. One decision was the adoption—or not—of slavery. Some states decided to keep slavery. Others did not.

DECLARATION OF INDEPENDENCE, JULY 4th, 1776.

1. What goal did the states have under the Constitution?
   a. to become stronger
   b. to promise rights to everyone
   c. to become united
   d. all the above

2. Look at the image. Who are the three characters in this cartoon??
   a. a British nobleman, Abraham Lincoln, Uncle Tom
   b. a Frenchman, George Washington, Uncle Sam
   c. a British nobleman, George Washington, Uncle Sam
   d. a Spanish person, George Washington, Uncle Sam

3. In 1789, where did the United States allow slaves?
   a. everywhere within it
   b. only in some states
   c. nowhere within it
   d. only in Northern states

Name: _____ **Date:** _____

Directions: Read the text, and answer the questions.

In 1820, the Missouri Compromise allowed each state to decide to have slavery or not. Generally, Southern states voted for slavery. Those in the North did not. Congress agreed to try to keep a balance between free and slave states.

Then, in 1854, the Kansas-Nebraska Act changed everything. Two new territories were created. They could decide on slavery. Some people, such as John Brown, opposed slavery. Others thought it was necessary. The conflict brought about many deaths. This was known as "Bleeding Kansas."

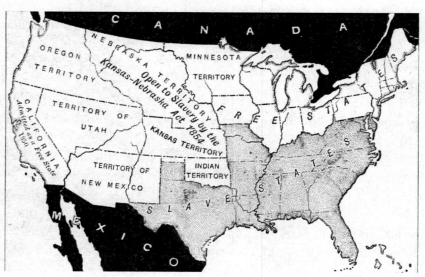

Civics

1. Based on the text, why was slavery allowed in some states? Circle all that apply.
   a. because of the Missouri Compromise
   b. because the citizens voted for slavery
   c. because Northerners wanted slaves
   d. because the central government approved

2. Why did Kansas become known as "Bleeding Kansas"?
   a. A lot of people were sick.
   b. Different opinions about slavery led to deaths.
   c. People in Kansas fought over land.
   d. The territory was a wild place.

3. What bothered Northerners about the Kansas-Nebraska Act?

   _____

   _____

   _____

Civics

Name:_____ Date:_____

Directions: Look at the map, and answer the questions.

an 1861 map during the American Civil War

1. Look at the titles at the top of the map. Who might be helped by sales of this map?

   a. sick and wounded Union soldiers

   b. sick and wounded southern soldiers

   c. a New England printing house

   d. runaway slaves from the South

2. On what was this map based?

   a. Confederate States data

   b. U.S. Army information

   c. the 1860 U.S. Census

   d. research by abolitionists

Name: _____ **Date:** _____

Directions: Read the text, and look at the images. Answer the questions.

The Fugitive Slave Act was passed in 1850. It said that all runaway slaves had to be returned to their owners. Anyone found helping them would be fined. If caught as a slave, a person had no right to a trial. There would be no investigation. This law made anti-slavery people very angry. They did not want to follow it. They were more likely to help runaways flee.

$200 Reward.

RANAWAY from the subscriber, on the night of Thursday, the 30th of Sepember,

FIVE NEGRO SLAVES,

To-wit: one Negro man, his wife, and three children.

reward poster for runaway slaves

a runaway slave in hiding

1. What did the Fugitive Slave Act do? Circle all that apply.

   a. It punished people who helped runaway slaves.

   b. It strengthened the rights of slaves.

   c. It gave slaves a right to a trial.

   d. It angered anti-slavery people.

2. Why did slave owners create these types of posters?

   _____

   _____

   _____

3. The people who helped slaves broke the law. Is it ever right to break the law? Why or why not?

   _____

   _____

   _____

Civics

Name: _____ **Date:** _____

Directions: Read the chart, and answer the questions.

Changes to the Constitution		
Amendment	**Date Approved**	**What the Amendment Did**
13th Amendment	1865	made slavery illegal
14th Amendment	1868	defined who are American citizens and forbade states from limiting their human rights
15th Amendment	1870	granted the right to vote to all men, regardless of color, race, or earlier condition

1. How did these changes to the Constitution improve life for Americans?

_____

_____

_____

_____

_____

_____

_____

_____

_____

_____

Name: _____ **Date:** _____

Directions: Read the text, and look at the image. Answer the questions.

Enslaved people sometimes ran away from their masters. Some people helped them. These friends formed the Underground Railroad. They were often called "conductors."

However, they were not usually on a railroad with tracks and engines. They were not usually underground, either.

Runaway slaves took many routes to freedom. They fled north, west, and even to Mexico. Quakers and other supporters protected them. They hid them in safe houses. Many people in the North helped guide them.

the Underground Railroad

Geography

1. How was the Underground Railroad like a regular railroad?

   a. It had tracks.

   b. It had an engine.

   c. It had coaches.

   d. It moved people.

2. In what ways was the railroad underground? Circle all that apply.

   a. It operated against the law.

   b. It worked in tunnels.

   c. It worked in secret.

   d. It was rooted in local towns.

3. What role did the railroad conductors play?

   a. They helped runaway slaves to freedom.

   b. They traveled on a railroad with slaves.

   c. They collected tickets for the ride.

   d. They conducted the music for the slaves.

Name: _____ **Date:** _____

Geography

Directions: Read the text, study the map, and answer the questions.

Fleeing slaves traveled by foot. They hid in wagons and carts. They took boats down rivers and across lakes. The unchanging North Star helped guide them. They often looked at a group of stars to find it. They called the stars the "Drinking Gourd."

But where was freedom? The Underground Railroad had a great many routes. For safety, most guides knew only their small part of a route. Many freedom seekers headed north. As many as 100,000 people escaped to what is now Canada between 1800 and 1865.

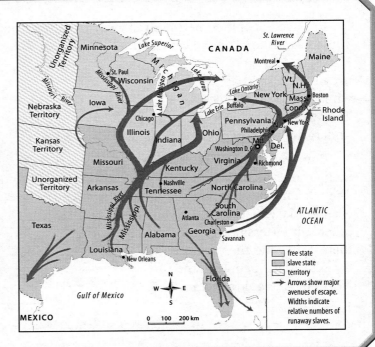

1. How did the night sky help the freedom seekers?
   a. The darkness made them feel safe.
   b. They told stories about the stars.
   c. The North Star provided direction.
   d. The light helped them to see.

2. Based on the text, how did the freedom seekers travel?
   a. by trains, by wagons, by tunnels
   b. on foot, by wagons, by boats
   c. on tracks, by water, on foot
   d. by tunnels, by trains, by ships

3. Use a finger to trace the northbound routes on the map. Where did most escaping slaves cross into Canada?
   a. from the state of Ohio
   b. from New York State
   c. from northern Michigan
   d. from northeastern states

Name: _____ **Date:** _____

Directions: Study the map, and answer the questions.

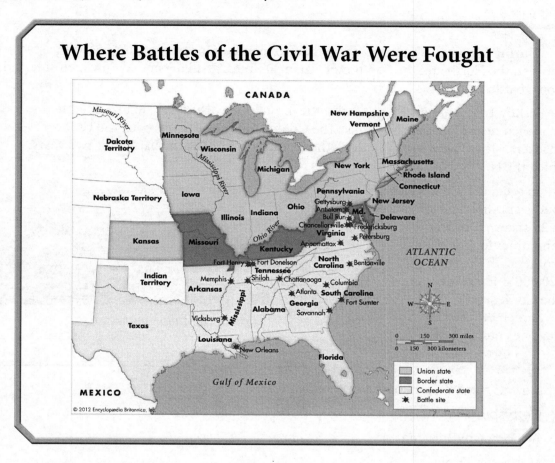

Where Battles of the Civil War Were Fought

1. In what part of the United States did most Civil War battles take place?
   a. Pacific Coast
   b. Midwest
   c. East
   d. Southwest

2. Why did several battles occurr near rivers and other bodies of water.

   _____

   _____

3. Near the end of the war, many battles took place in Virginia. Where is Virginia located? Why do you think so many battles took place there?

   _____

   _____

   _____

Geography

Name: _____ Date: _____

Directions: Read the text, and answer the questions.

During the Civil War, many areas changed hands. One city in Virginia was passed between the North and the South more than 70 times. It all depended on which side had won a battle.

In July 1861, soldiers fought the Battle of Bull Run. The war's first land battle happened near Manassas, Virginia. The Confederate army drove back the Union attackers. There were many battles. The South won most of the battles for two years. Then, the North started to win.

In total, the war lasted four years. Soldiers fought in 25 states. Brothers sometimes fought against brothers. In the end, 620,000 soldiers died. The Confederate States surrendered. The Union was one country again.

hospital for Union soldiers

1. Where was the first land battle of the Civil War?
   a. Gettysburg, Pennsylvania
   b. Appomattox, Virginia
   c. Manassas, Virginia
   d. Point of Rocks, Virginia

2. The South called the Battle of Bull Run the "Battle of Manassas." Why do you think the North's name for the battle is used?

   _____

   _____

3. Consider how a current map of the United States would look if the Confederates had won the Civil War. Explain.

   _____

   _____

   _____

© *Shell Education*

Name: _____ **Date:** _____

Directions: Study the map, and answer the question.

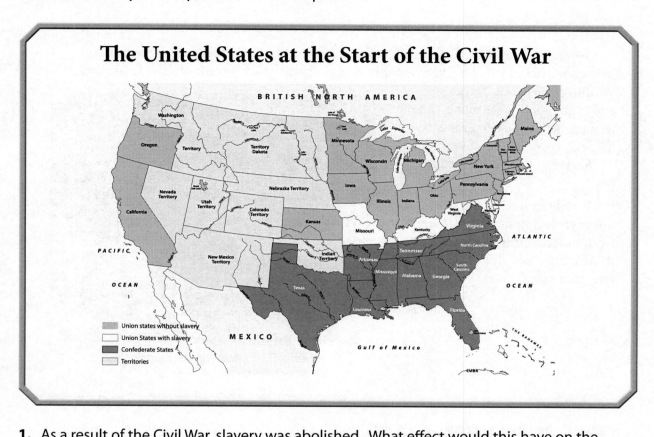

The United States at the Start of the Civil War

Union states without slavery
Union States with slavery
Confederate States
Territories

1. As a result of the Civil War, slavery was abolished. What effect would this have on the Northern and Southern states and territories as shown on the map?

Geography

Economics

Name:_____ Date:_____

Directions: Read the text, and answer the questions.

After the Civil War, America developed new industries. Steel mills were built to help construct railroads. Oil companies were created. New inventions made life easier. Washing machines, bicycles, and many tools were made. The telegraph and the telephone helped people keep in touch. In 1896, Henry Ford built his first car.

People moved to the cities. They worked in factories. People from other countries moved to America, too. This made America more diverse!

Henry Ford's first car, the Quadricycle

1. Why did the cities become very busy?
   a. Many more people arrived.
   b. Airplanes brought in people.
   c. People who lived in cities used new inventions.
   d. Cars created traffic problems.

2. Why did people work in factories?
   a. They liked the short workdays.
   b. The environment was safe.
   c. The children had fun.
   d. Lots of factories offered work.

3. Why were people interested in coming to the United States?
   a. They came to enjoy new inventions.
   b. They came to work in the factories.
   c. They came to drive Henry Ford's cars.
   d. They came because ship fares were cheap.

Name: _____ **Date:** _____

Directions: Read the text, and answer the questions.

By 1860, all the cities in the North and the Midwest were connected by railroad tracks. This helped the economy because crops and animals could be sent throughout these areas. During the Civil War, the North used trains to move its troops. The South had fewer rail lines.

After the Civil War, railroads were improved. By 1869, the first railroad to go from east to west was finished. People took it west to start farms and ranches. Food and cattle were sent by rail, too.

train station in Minnesota

first transcontinental railroad, 1869

1. What was the main reason railroads were built?
   a. to connect the North with the South
   b. to connect the United States with Canada
   c. to connect the North with the Midwest
   d. to help Americans reach Mexico

2. How did railroads improve the economy?
   a. People were able to reach the sea.
   b. They provided safer travel.
   c. Farmers could ship crops to sell.
   d. People took holiday trips west.

3. Why did people use western trails less after the Civil War? Circle all that apply.
   a. The wagons were all broken.
   b. Trains crossed the land faster.
   c. Troops no longer needed supplies.
   d. Trains carried freight more easily.

Economics

Name: _____ **Date:** _____

Directions: Look at the photo, and read the caption. Answer the questions.

Field hands were former slaves who now worked for bosses instead of for owners.

1. The photo of the field was taken a few decades after the Civil War. What has changed? What has stayed the same?

_____

_____

_____

_____

_____

_____

2. Who do you think owns this land? What makes you think that?

_____

_____

_____

_____

_____

_____

Name:_____ **Date:**_____

Directions: Read the text, look at the image, and answer the questions.

Economics

For thousands of years, all farm work was done by physical labor. People used small tools, such as shovels and pitchforks. Even before the Civil War, though, that began to change. Americans invented tools and then machines to make farm work easier. Eli Whitney's cotton gin reduced the work of separating seeds from fibers. John Deere designed a steel plow, which was easier to clean than a wooden plow. When tractors and combines were invented, farmers could produce more crops. Machines never got tired, so fewer horses were needed.

threshing machine, late 1800s

1. Which answer is NOT correct?

   a. The machines lightened the work.

   b. The machines never got tired.

   c. The machines replaced horses.

   d. The machines were all easy to clean.

2. Look at the image of an old threshing machine. How did new tools and machines reduce the need for horses?

   _____

   _____

   _____

3. What do you use to make your life easier? Why?

   _____

   _____

   _____

Economics

Name: _____ **Date:** _____

Directions: Look at the images, and answer the question.

ruins in Richmond, Virginia

a Southern railroad after the Civil War

1. Based on the images, what kind of damages were caused by the Civil War? How might this have affected the South's economy?

_____

_____

_____

_____

_____

_____

_____

_____

ANSWER KEY *(cont.)*

Week 1—History

Day 1
1. c
2. a
3. c
4. c

Day 2
1. c
2. b
3. Responses will vary.

Day 3
1. b
2. d
3. Northwest, California, Northeast Woodland; each hunted whales that live in oceans.

Day 4
1. b
2. Responses will vary but may include dry, easy to carry, high in protein.
3. Responses will vary but may include energy bar, trail mix.

Day 5
1. Responses will vary but may include Potlatch and Christmas.

Week 2—Civics

Day 1
1. c
2. d
3. c
4. Responses will vary but may include "Star-Spangled Banner"

Day 2
1. b
2. c
3. c
4. Responses will vary but may include a promise to our country, feeling of pride in United States.

Day 3
1. c
2. b
3. Responses will vary but may include looking at the flag after a battle that was won.

Day 4
1. Responses will vary but may include spacious skies, amber waves, purple mountains, fruited plain, and shining sea.
2. Responses will vary but may include majesties, America, God shed His grace, brotherhood, freedom, liberty, and patriot.
3. Responses will vary but may include spacious skies, waves of grain, purple mountains, fruited plain, and shining seas.

Day 5
1. Responses will vary.

Week 3—Geography

Day 1
1. d
2. b
3. a, c

Day 2
1. c
2. a
3. d

Day 3
1. c
2. a
3. Responses will vary but may include small animals, birds, seeds, roots, cacti, insects, berries, nuts, plants, elk, and deer.

Day 4
1. b
2. Responses will vary.
3. Responses will vary.

ANSWER KEY *(cont.)*

Day 5

1. Responses will vary but may include companion planning, nitrogen in soil, corn used nitrogen to grow.
2. Responses will vary but may include corn chowder, bean chilli, and squash soup.

Week 4—Economics

Day 1

1. d
2. a
3. c
4. a

Day 2

1. c
2. b
3. Responses will vary but may include AD 200 and AD 1565.

Day 3

1. a
2. c
3. d

Day 4

1. b
2. Responses will vary but may include barbecue or open wood fire.
3. Responses will vary but may include hamburgers, hot dogs, etc.

Day 5

1. Responses will vary but may include bark gathered for houses, corn drying for food, and animal hides used as clothes.

Week 5—History

Day 1

1. d
2. c
3. a
4. b

Day 2

1. b
2. a
3. a
4. b

Day 3

1. c
2. b
3. Responses will vary but may include the following: European clothing—hats, shoes, socks, coats, shirts; American Indians—blankets/robes, sandals, boots, loincloths, headdresses with feathers, jewelry; both—footwear.

Day 4

1. d
2. b
3. Responses will vary.

Day 5

1. Responses will vary but may include that the American Indians feared Columbus's power, weapons, etc.; Columbus saw trade possibilities with the American Indians.

Week 6—Civics

Day 1

1. b
2. b
3. d

Day 2

1. d
2. b
3. c
4. Responses will vary.

ANSWER KEY *(cont.)*

Day 3
1. a, b
2. Responses will vary but may include that the fort can be protected from all sides.

Day 4
1. b, d
2. Responses will vary but may include represents welcome at gateway to the United States, liberty, light of freedom, and freedom from injustice.
3. Responses will vary.

Day 5
1. Responses will vary but may include distance from home, cost, travel time, and personal preference.

Week 7—Geography

Day 1
1. b
2. a
3. c

Day 2
1. a
2. d
3. c

Day 3
1. b
2. c
3. Responses will vary but may include ability to read and write, and knowledge of mathematics and astronomy.

Day 4
1. b
2. c
3. Responses will vary but may include by boat (Mississippi River), plane, train, and car.

Day 5
1. Responses will vary but may include trees available to build a house, near water for travel, drinking, and food.

Week 8—Economics

Day 1
1. d
2. b
3. c

Day 2
1. b
2. a
3. d

Day 3
1. b
2. a
3. Responses will vary but may include wheat, rice, barley, and oats; farmers would grow crops and raise livestock, such as cattle, pigs, sheep, and horses; flour would be made from grains.

Day 4
1. c
2. Responses will vary but may include wheat, rice, citrus fruit, peaches, etc.
3. Responses will vary but may include diseases such as smallpox, measles, influenza, and typhus.

Day 5
1. Responses will vary.

Week 9—History

Day 1
1. d
2. b
3. c

Day 2
1. b
2. c
3. a

Day 3
1. b
2. d
3. Responses will vary but may include that the Pilgrims probably would not survive.

Day 4

1. a
2. Responses will vary but may include women: doing laundry, cooking; men: bringing goods to shore on boat, protection by soldiers.
3. Responses will vary.

Day 5

1. Document at center; bible nearby; Pilgrims in awe of idea; most attention on document

Week 10—Civics

Day 1

1. c
2. d
3. a, c

Day 2

1. b
2. a
3. d

Day 3

1. c
2. a
3. Responses will vary but may talk about taxes, budget, and laws.

Day 4

1. d
2. Responses will vary but may include that he respected them; he listened to them; he believed people should have freedoms.
3. Responses will vary.

Day 5

1. Responses will vary.

Week 11—Geography

Day 1

1. b
2. d
3. a

Day 2

1. c
2. d
3. d

Day 3

1. a
2. b
3. Responses will vary.

Day 4

1. d
2. Responses will vary but may include build houses, farm, and be a carpenter.
3. Responses will vary.

Day 5

1. Check student maps for accuracy.

Week 12—Economics

Day 1

1. b
2. d
3. c
4. d

Day 2

1. b
2. c
3. b
4. Responses will vary but may include books, newspapers, posters, and pamphlets.

Day 3

1. b
2. Responses will vary but may include wood, axes, rope, saws, and wooden horses.
3. Responses will vary but may include access to water for boat launching, and trees for wood.

Day 4

1. d
2. Responses will vary.
3. Responses will vary.

ANSWER KEY (cont.)

Day 5

1. Responses will vary but may include the following: New England Colonies: fish, naval stores, shipbuilding, lumber, beaver fur, and corn; Middle Colonies: wheat, staves, beaver fur, shipbuilding, fish, corn, hemp, and lumber; Southern Colonies: hides, rice, indigo, tobacco, naval stores, and lumber.

Week 13—History

Day 1

1. c
2. b
3. a, c

Day 2

1. c
2. b
3. a

Day 3

1. b, d
2. Responses will vary but may include to state their unhappiness with Britain's taxes; to stop buying British goods; to talk about forming a national government.
3. Responses will vary but may include to form a national government; appoint a commander for the army; organize militia; make plans to separate from Britain.

Day 4

1. b, c, d
2. a
3. Responses will vary but may include be humble, listen to others, etc.

Day 5

1. Responses will vary.

Week 14—Civics

Day 1

1. c
2. a
3. d

Day 2

1. b
2. c
3. c

Day 3

1. d
2. Responses will vary but should include liberty and freedom; they are very determined; they would die for the cause.
3. Responses will vary but may include always watching; doesn't surrender; hidden defenses; small but deadly weapons; and gives warning before attack.

Day 4

1. c
2. d
3. Responses will vary.

Day 5

1. Responses will vary but may include the following: Patriots: wanted to break from Britain, wanted to govern themselves; Loyalists: didn't want to break with Britain, wanted to do business with Britain, thought British rule was best; both: pay high taxes, could not trade with whom they wanted, had to house and feed British soldiers.

Week 15—Geography

Day 1

1. Located on map
2. b
3. b

Day 2

1. b
2. c
3. Disputed area is the land between that held by the British and the French; each country wanted this land.

ANSWER KEY *(cont.)*

Day 3
1. c
2. d
3. Responses will vary but may include that the travel lines from the three continents form the shape of a triangle; depended on shipping, need for products, markets among these continents.

Day 4
1. c
2. c
3. Responses will vary.

Day 5
4. Responses will vary but may include the following: Plantation Owner: big home, verandas, fancy clothes, didn't work, few people lived in house; Slaves: small home, no veranda, plain clothes, many people lived in home; Both: had a home and family.

Week 16—Economics

Day 1
1. a, d
2. a
3. a
4. d

Day 2
1. c
2. a
3. Responses will vary but may include to control and get taxes from the colonies.

Day 3
1. c
2. d
3. b
4. Virginia had over 182,000 enslaved people, compared to 5,561 for Pennsylvania; responses will vary but may include that more cotton plantations were in Virginia.

Day 4
1. b
2. c
3. Responses will vary.

Day 5
1. Responses will vary but may include ruined crates of tea; threw crates of tea into Boston Harbor; disguised as American Indians; ruining tea that could be sold; taxes could not be collected by the British.

Week 17—History

Day 1
1. b, d
2. c
3. d

Day 2
1. b
2. d
3. Responses will vary but may include joined the army when no women were allowed; was one of the first women in the American army; felt strongly enough about duty to her country to join in secret; fought in battle; and showed leadership in the army.

Day 3
1. d
2. Responses will vary but may include convinced France to join the Patriots in war; helped negotiate Treaty of Paris; and helped write the Constitution.
3. Responses will vary but may include owned *Pennsylvania Gazette* newspaper; worked for the Committee of Secret Correspondence; helped write the draft of the Declaration of Independence; helped write the Constitution; and helped write the Treaty of Paris.

ANSWER KEY *(cont.)*

Day 4
1. b
2. Responses will vary but may include that Hale was the first American spy to die in service; and his statue is a reminder of liberty and patriotism for Americans.
3. Responses will vary.

Day 5
1. Responses will vary but may include that they would run away; they might pretend to be patriots; and they might spy for the British.

Week 18—Civics

Day 1
1. d
2. b
3. a, b, c

Day 2
1. b
2. d
3. c

Day 3
1. b
2. a
3. Responses will vary but may include to inform the population, those who could read and those who could not.

Day 4
1. c
2. Responses will vary but may include that they did not acknowledge the country; they were ashamed of not winning the war; and they were not proud to sit for picture after such a defeat.
3. Responses will vary.

Day 5
1. Responses will vary but should include the following: the three branches of government are Legislative, Executive, and Judicial; the branches are separated to make sure no one has too much power.

Week 19—Geography

Day 1
1. b
2. c. See map.
3. a

Day 2
1. c
2. d
3. Responses should be Cahokia, Kaskaskia, Vincennes, and Fort Henry.

Day 3
1. a. See map.
2. See map. Responses will vary but may include he strength of the British Navy; its ability to supply troops; and the fact that Boston was surrounded
3. b, c

Day 4
1. d
2. Responses will vary but may include direct armies to surround the British; battle to take place on flat land; be ready to attack in waves.
3. Responses will vary.

Day 5
1. Responses will vary but may include the following: Then, U.S. 1777 flag: 13 stars in circle on blue background representing number of states; now, U.S. flag: 50 stars on blue background representing number of states; both: 13 stripes, 7 red, 6 white, white stars on blue background, each star represents a state.

Week 20—Economics

Day 1
1. b
2. c
3. a

Day 2
1. c
2. a
3. b

ANSWER KEY (cont.)

Day 3
1. c
2. b
3. Reponses will vary but may include that Americans did not want to pay more taxes; and the debt continued to rise.

Day 4
1. a
2. c
3. Responses will vary but may include paper, which it is light and easy to carry.

Day 5
1. Responses will vary but may include lthat modern coins have images of presidents, national monuments, slogans, and symbols.

Week 21—History

Day 1
1. a
2. d
3. Responses will vary but may include that the colonies joined together as the United States.

Day 2
1. b
2. c
3. d

Day 3
1. d
2. c
3. Responses will vary but may include that there were a lot of slaves in America; it was common practice to have slaves; and it was not against the law to have slaves.

Day 4
1. c
2. Responses will vary but may include the right to capture runaway slaves.
3. Responses will vary.

Day 5
1. Responses will vary.

Week 22—Civics

Day 1
1. d
2. d
3. a, c

Day 2
1. b
2. c
3. a

Day 3
1. c
2. a
3. Responses will vary but should include freedoms of religion, speech, the press, peaceful assembly, and to be heard.

Day 4
1. c
2. Responses will vary but may include to be a good person; take part in politics; make sure governments act responsibly; engage in community life.
3. Responses will vary.

Day 5.
1. Responses will vary.

Week 23—Geography

Day 1
1. b
2. a
3. d

Day 2
1. b
2. a, c
3. a

ANSWER KEY *(cont.)*

Day 3
1. b
2. Responses will vary but may include that work was done manually; no machines; harvesting needed to be done quickly when the crop was ready to pick; there was a lot of work to do because of the size of the fields.
3. Responses will vary but may include long days; hard work; cruel overseers; no freedom; no education; worked every day; and could be sold.

Day 4
1. d
2. Responses will vary but may include that cotton was grown in those states.
3. Responses will vary but may include that plantations were in those states; enslaved people were needed to do the work on the plantations; it was a part of the Confederate states' economy.

Day 5
1. Responses will vary but should include the following: Britain: give up forts in Northwest Territory, Indians told not to attack, paid for 250 ships; United States: agreed not to help France fight Britain, paid debts from revolution; both: U.S.-Canada border, trade between both countries.

Week 24—Economics

Day 1
1. b
2. c
3. a

Day 2
1. c
2. b
3. Responses will vary but may include that speed of mills meant that more flour was ground more cheaply; savings for consumers; and more profits for mill owners.

Day 3
1. b
2. Responses will vary but may include flour, corn, wheat, potatoes, tobacco, cotton, pigs, cattle, chickens, and wood from the boat once it reached downstream.
3. Responses will vary but may include that boats were too heavy to row upstream; power to move boats had not been invented yet; and it was easier and quicker to come home alone and build another boat.

Day 4
1. a, b
2. Responses will vary but may include that Slater is said to be the founder of the Industrial Revolution in America.
3. Responses will vary but may include cutting grass, babysitting, washing cars, etc.

Day 5
1. Reponses will vary. Responses could include: faster to plant seeds, can plant seeds alone, plant seeds in one pass, fewer workers needed to farm.

Week 25—History

Day 1
1. a
2. b
3. a, c

Day 2
1. d
2. a, b, c
3. a, c, d

ANSWER KEY *(cont.)*

Day 3
1. a
2. b
3. Responses will vary but may include that Jefferson set a goal to build a university; setting a goal is hopeful.

Day 4
1. Responses will vary
2. Responses will vary but may include that American Indians were forced from their lands; some died as they moved to their new location; some became very ill; and they were sad.

Day 5
1. Responses will vary but should include that the Missouri Compromise of 1820 meant that no other state could become a slave state.

Week 26—Civics

Day 1
1. c
2. c
3. d

Day 2
1. d
2. b
3. Responses will vary but may include the use of capital letters, EXTRA edition, and catch words such as *Germany*, and *surrendered*.

Day 3
1. c
2. Responses will vary but may include a list of specific world leader names; past, present, and future events; independence; present-day leaders; and hopes for future as a country.
3. Responses will vary but may include names of historical figures; personal reasons for choices; qualities admired; and questions to ask.

Day 4
1. a
2. b (Caribbean is considered part of North America)
3. Responses will vary but may include that Columbus did not discover the United States; but some Americans connect to Columbus's Italian heritage.

Day 5
1. Responses will vary but may include that all people are created equal; all Americans can have a good life, get along with each other and respect others; race, creed, and/or gender; should not influence choices or ideas about how one lives or works.

Week 27—Geography

Day 1
1. a
2. c
3. d

Day 2
1. b, c, d
2. a, b, c
3. d

Day 3
1. b
2. c
3. Responses will vary but may include considerations such as length; ability to travel; directions across country; farmland/lifestyle opportunities, etc.

Day 4
1. d
2. a, c, d
3. Responses will vary but may include that Clark wanted to leave his mark.

Day 5

1. Responses will vary but may include that the United States expanded its territory by purchasing, negotiating (some land ceded), and fighting other countries to claim land.

Week 28—Economics

Day 1

1. b
2. a
3. c

Day 2

1. d
2. a, b, c
3. Responses will vary but may include that their families were poor and needed the money.

Day 3

1. a
2. Responses will vary.

Day 4

1. a
2. 34 coins (34 half-pennies make 17¢)
3. Responses will vary but should include that land was plentiful; one must provide feed and care to animals; animals were not as plentiful.
4. 85¢ (coffee—17¢ x 5); 40¢ (sugar—20¢ x 2) = $1.25.

Day 5

1. Responses will vary.

Week 29—History

Day 1

1. b
2. a
3. Responses will vary but should include that 1,000 people, 100 wagons, and 5,000 cattle and oxen traveled 2,000 miles in 1843.

Day 2

1. b, d
2. a, d
3. b

Day 3

1. Responses will vary but may include that forts were military posts; provided protection, health aid, food/water, directions, mail, etc.
2. Responses will vary but may include that they camped in circle formation to protect selves/animals from danger; small circles kept people closer to each other; only a few animals can be in middle of small circle; large circle might cause stampede; other possible dangers.

Day 4

1. d
2. a
3. Responses will vary but may include that railroads/trains made the trip west faster and easier compared to wagon travel.

Day 5

1. Responses will vary but may include that travelers depleted/shot buffalo herds, burned firewood, and brought disease; and oxen overgrazed prairie grass.

Week 30—Civics

Day 1

1. a
2. b
3. Responses will vary but may include that Monroe disliked slavery, despite owning slaves himself.

Day 2

1. a
2. a, d
3. b

Day 3

1. a
2. b, d
3. Responses will vary but may include warning black people and fugitive slaves of possible kidnapping by slave catchers and others who would force them into (back into) slavery.

Day 4

1. a
2. Responses will vary but may include that the people wanted slavery to end.

Day 5

1. Responses should include the following: federalists: 1, 4; anti-federalists: 2, 3

Week 31—Geography

Day 1

1. c
2. b
3. d

Day 2

1. b
2. c
3. d

Day 3

1. a, b, c
2. Missouri, Nebraska, Wyoming, Utah, and Nevada
3. Responses will vary.

Day 4

1. a, d
2. b
3. Responses will vary.

Day 5

1. Responses will vary.

Week 32—Economics

Day 1

1. a, c
2. a
3. d

Day 2

1. d
2. c
3. Responses will vary.

Day 3

1. b
2. a
3. Responses will vary but may include the need to keep horses fresh and healthy; good profits from service meant that they could afford more stations, fresh horses, etc.

Day 4

1. d
2. c
3. Responses will vary but may include the telegraph, pony express, etc.

Day 5

1. Responses will vary.

Week 33—Economics

Day 1

1. c
2. b
3. c

Day 2

1. b
2. c
3. Responses will vary but may include that freedom and equality are incompatible with slavery.

Day 3

1. Responses will vary but may include that pro-slavery advocates needed to dismiss the humanity of slaves.
2. Responses will vary but may include that the image made people feel guilty and angry about slavery.

ANSWER KEY (cont.)

Day 4
1. b
2. Responses will vary but should include that Confederate army could surround the fort; the Union army had no way to get more supplies since it was on water.
3. Responses will vary.

Day 5
1. Responses will vary but may include that the South needed slaves for its economy; the North hated slavery.

Week 34—Civics

Day 1
1. d
2. c
3. b

Day 2
1. a, b
2. b
3. Responses will vary but may include that vote on slavery was a step backwards; Northerners did not accept the right to choose slavery; and they wanted all Northern states to be free.

Day 3
1. a
2. c

Day 4
1. a, d
2. Responses will vary but may include that slaves were valuable property.
3. Responses will vary but may include civil disobedience, nonviolence, etc.

Day 5
1. Responses will vary but may include that the 13th Amendment made slavery illegal and freed millions; the 14th Amendment made ex-slaves citizens and gave them rights they never had before; the 15th Amendment gave male African Americans the right to vote.

Week 35—Geography

Day 1
1. d
2. a, c
3. a

Day 2
1. c
2. b
3. d

Day 3
1. c
2. Responses will vary but may include that water was important for transportation; it could also be a barrier.
3. Responses will vary but may include that battles in Virginia were in the center of the country, close to the capital of Washington, D.C.

Day 4
1. c
2. Responses will vary but should include that the North got to name the battle because it won the war and wrote the history.
3. Responses will vary but may include that the United States would not be a single country; it could be divided into North and South and possibly other divisions in the West.

Day 5
1. Responses will vary but may include that the end of slavery freed millions of African Americans; Reconstruction and Jim Crow laws curtailed their civil rights.

Week 36—Economics

Day 1
1. a
2. d
3. b

Day 2

1. c
2. c
3. b, d

Day 3

1. Responses will vary but may include that slaves worked without pay, but field hands worked for wages; sharecroppers paid part of the crop as rent.
2. Responses will vary but should include that the boss owned the land; it could be the person on the horse or on the tractor/wagon.

Day 4

1. d
2. Responses will vary.
3. Responses will vary.

Day 5

1. Responses will vary.

POLITICAL MAP OF THE UNITED STATES

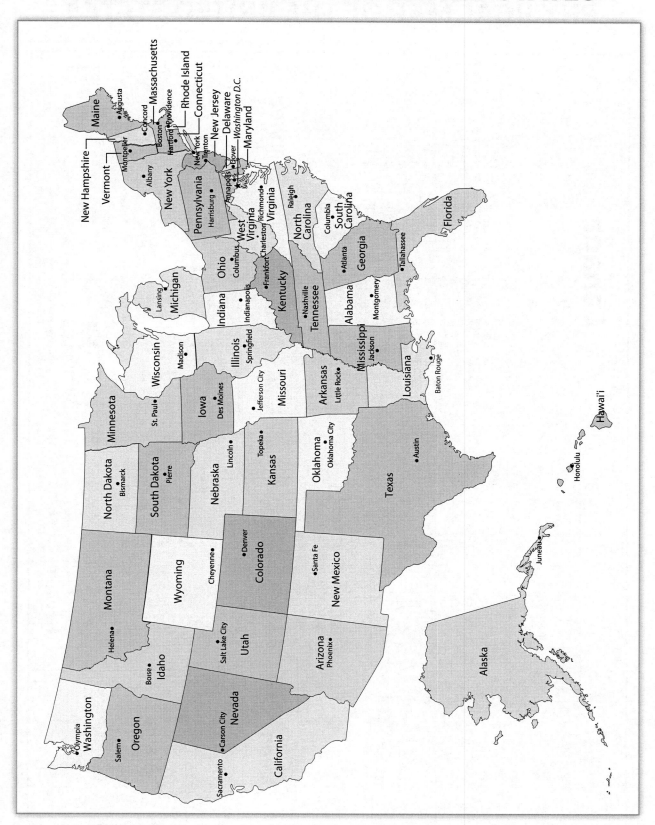

PHYSICAL MAP OF THE UNITED STATES

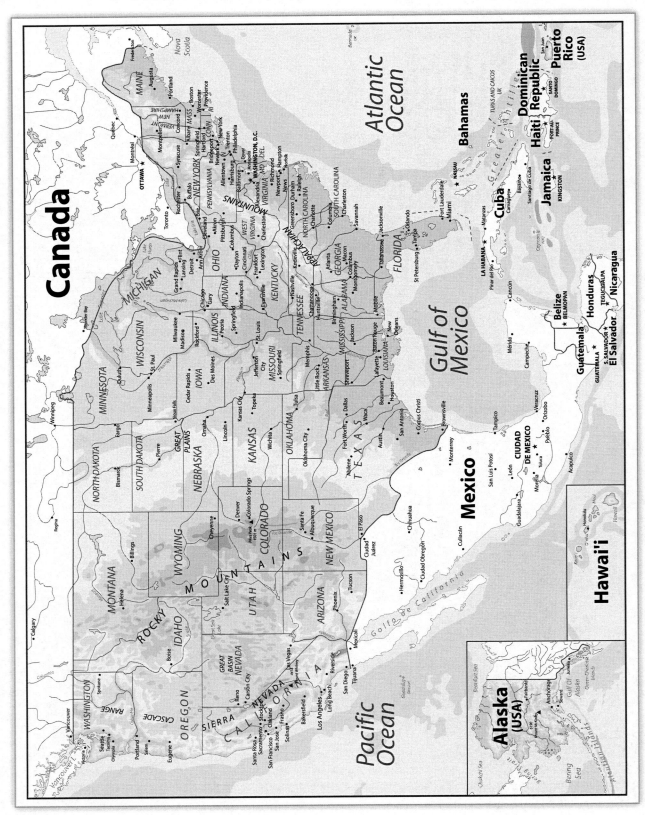

WORLD MAP

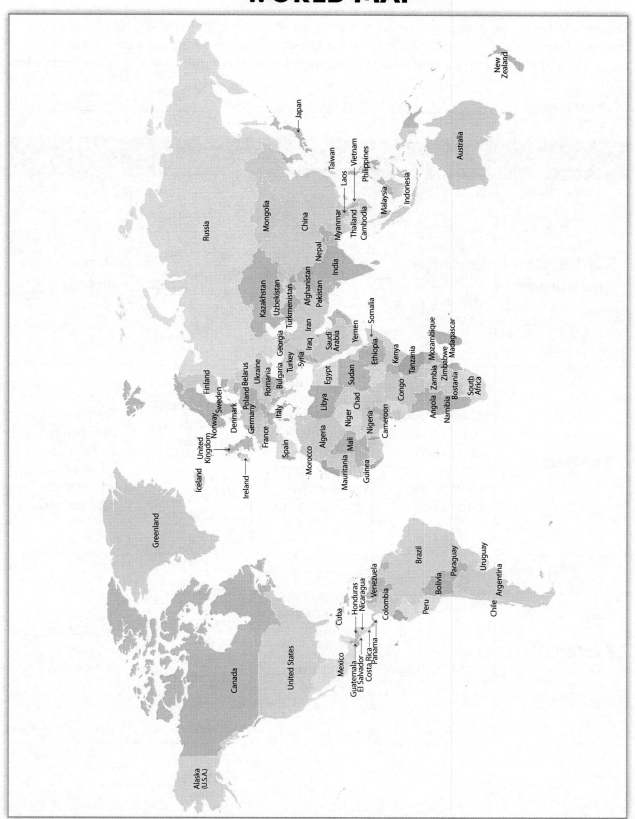

Response Rubric

Teacher Directions: The answer key provides answers for the multiple-choice and short-answer questions. This rubric can be used for any open-ended questions where student responses vary. Evaluate student work to determine how many points out of 12 students earn.

Student Name: _____

	4 Points	3 Points	2 Points	1 Point
Content Knowledge	Gives right answers. Answers are based on text and prior knowledge.	Gives right answers based on text.	Gives mostly right answers based on text.	Gives incorrect answers.
Analysis	Thinks about the content, and draws strong inferences/ conclusions.	Thinks about the content, and draws mostly correct inferences/ conclusions.	Thinks about the content, and draws somewhat correct inferences/ conclusions.	Thinks about the content, and draws incorrect inferences/ conclusions.
Explanation	Explains and supports answers fully.	Explains and supports answers with some evidence.	Explains and supports answers with little evidence.	Provides no support for answers.

Total: _____

Practice Page Item Analysis

Teacher Directions: Record how many multiple-choice questions students answered correctly. Then, record their rubric totals for Day 5. Total the four weeks of scores, and record that number in the Overall column.

Circle Week Range: 1–4 5–8 9–12 13–16 17–20 21–24 25–28 29–32 33–36						
Student Name	**Day 1** Text Analysis	**Day 2** Text Analysis	**Day 3** Primary Source or Visual Text	**Day 4** Making Connections	**Day 5** Synthesis and Application	**Overall**
Ryan	1, 2, 2, 3	2, 2, 2, 2	2, 2, 1, 2	1, 1, 2, 1	12, 10, 12, 12	73

Student Item Analysis By Discipline

Teacher Directions: Record how many multiple-choice questions students answered correctly. Then, record their rubric totals for Day 5. Total the four weeks of scores, and record that number in the Overall column.

Student Name:

History Weeks	Day 1 Text Analysis	Day 2 Text Analysis	Day 3 Primary Source or Visual Text	Day 4 Making Connections	Day 5 Synthesis and Application	Overall
1						
5						
9						
13						
17						
21						
25						
29						
33						
Civics Weeks	Day 1 Text Analysis	Day 2 Text Analysis	Day 3 Primary Source or Visual Text	Day 4 Making Connections	Day 5 Synthesis and Application	Overall
2						
6						
10						
14						
18						
22						
26						
30						
34						

Student Item Analysis By Discipline *(cont.)*

Student Name:						
Geography Weeks	**Day 1** Text Analysis	**Day 2** Text Analysis	**Day 3** Primary Source or Visual Text	**Day 4** Making Connections	**Day 5** Synthesis and Application	**Overall**
3						
7						
11						
15						
19						
23						
27						
31						
35						
Economics Weeks	**Day 1** Text Analysis	**Day 2** Text Analysis	**Day 3** Primary Source or Visual Text	**Day 4** Making Connections	**Day 5** Synthesis and Application	**Overall**
4						
8						
12						
16						
20						
24						
28						
32						
36						

Digital Resources

To access the digital resources, go to this website and enter the following code: 50650780.
www.teachercreatedmaterials.com/administrators/download-files/

Rubric and Analysis Sheets

Resource	Filename
Response Rubric	responserubric.pdf
Practice Page Item Analysis	itemanalysis.pdf
	itemanalysis.docx
	itemanalysis.xlsx
Student Item Analysis by Discipline	socialstudiesanalysis.pdf
	socialstudiesanalysis.docx
	socialstudiesanalysis.xlsx

Standards and Themes

Resource	Filename
Weekly Topics and Themes	topicsthemes.pdf
Standards Charts	standards.pdf